There's no business
like social business

There's no business like social business

How to be socially enterprising

Liam Black and Jeremy Nicholls

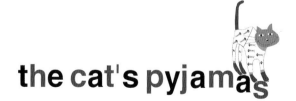

the cat's pyjamas

First published in the United Kingdom in 2004 by
the Cat's Pyjamas

Text copyright © the Cat's Pyjamas 2004

Design and layout copyright © Different Angle 2004

Photography copyright © Different Angle

ISBN 0 9547101 0 X

Concept, design, photography and production
by Different Angle

The Cat's Pyjamas
Atlantic Way
Brunswick Business Park
Liverpool L3 4BE
United Kingdom

www.the-cats-pyjamas.com

We would like to thank all the people featured in this book who gave so generously of their time and insights; to the Small Business Service – in particular Maria Kenyon – for getting behind us; to our informal editorial team of Barbara, Tim, Alison, Shaun, Tony, Erik, Sara, and Anne Marie; and to Paul Bate of Different Angle whose design brilliance is matched only by his patience and good humour.

Contents

"The future of the world lies in the hands of these market-based social entrepreneurs. We cannot combat poverty within the orthodoxy of capitalism practiced today. Economic theory has not provided us with any alternative to this familiar model but I argue that we can create a powerful alternative: a social-consciousness-driven private sector, created by social entrepreneurs."

Muhammad Yunus,
founder of the Grameen Bank
in Bangladesh, whose mission
is to eradicate poverty from
the entire world.

Introduction

S ocial enterprise is a state of mind. It's about values, a passion for social justice and equity matched by the drive to create self-sufficient, market facing businesses. Our vision is of a community of thriving businesses, part of the enterprise economy, generating services and products which reduce inequality and create new opportunities with people who are usually left out.

This book has been inspired by the creativity and energy of the many social entrepreneurs throughout the world searching for business solutions to social and environmental challenges.

We launched the Cat's Pyjamas in February 2000 to help people get to the heart of the cultures of social businesses, businesses which are making money at the same time as addressing social issues such as creating opportunities for unemployed people, supporting the homeless or tackling environmental issues.

Since then we have met hundreds of people from all over the country and beyond, involved in setting up, managing, governing, funding, investing in, consulting with, or working in social enterprises of all shapes and sizes and ownership models. We have been by turns moved, impressed, challenged, appalled, baffled and enthused by what we have seen and heard. There is some amazing socially entrepreneurial stuff going on out there on every continent. From inner city Liverpool and San Francisco, to the townships of South Africa and the barrios of Latin America, by way of the rural villages of India and Bangladesh, there is something very exciting afoot.

In the year we have been writing this book, the social entrepreneur landscape nationally and internationally, has been evolving quickly. In the United Kingdom, social enterprise is part of the Government's national policy agenda[1]. Internationally, the Schwab Foundation, Ashoka and the Skoll Foundation are driving a global strategy to network social entrepreneurs[2].

The Cat's Pyjamas provides well known social businesses in Britain with the space to be completely honest about the struggles and mistakes they have made so others can learn from them. We learn at least as much from peoples' mistakes and howlers as we do from their best practice. Our hosts love the chance to talk freely about the good old bad old days, or how they nearly went bust, without feeling they will be pounced on for letting the side down.

The purpose of this book is to offer practical advice and useful insights to those running or intending to start a social enterprise. This book addresses the big issues which come up again and again in conversations and arguments about social enterprise. Issues about ownership, leadership, verification, growth. It is a mixture of dispatches from our part of the frontline; a polemic and a showcase for what we think are some of the best in the business, and insights of leading social entrepreneurs. We have not become immersed in the philosophical

[1] www.dti.gov.uk/socialenterprise   [2] www.schwabfound.org   www.ashoka.org   www.skollfoundation.org

and ideological disputations that can beset the sector but, when important, we try to deal with them.

You won't agree with us on everything. Wouldn't that be boring and highly unlikely? Still less do we believe that this little book contains The Truth About Social Enterprise. We hope it will inform, provoke, and, who knows, inspire you. We will have succeeded if you find in the following pages anything which helps you deal better with the very challenging and complex privilege of running a social enterprise.

This book is principally aimed at people working in organisations in the economy seeking to manage a triple bottom line.

But we hope that what we write will be of interest to people running all sorts of businesses – including private ones – where values and people matter as much as profit.

Jeremy and Liam
Liverpool
March 2004

"... it is a fragile thing.... learning from others helps refine the light touch needed to deliver such a precious cargo."

Equity,
profit, proof
on being a social business

"*Hope is a state of mind, not of the world. Hope, in this deep and powerful sense, is not the same as joy that things are going well, or willingness to invest in enterprises that are obviously heading for success, but rather an ability to work for something because it is good.*"

Vaclav Havel

L et's start with a quiz.

Which of these organisations is a social enterprise?

1. Company A is based in one the country's poorest wards and makes products which save the lives of thousands of people every year. It does not carry out social reporting.

2. Company B's product has enabled thousands of homeless people to earn an income. It does not have a social report.

3. Since it started trading, Company C has made it possible for thousands of low income families to get good quality domestic furniture by offering people credit which they might otherwise have to get from loan sharks. It does not publish a social report.

4. Company D buys its products from sustainable sources and is a leader in developing recycling and reuse technologies and products. It employs locally and publishes a social report.

5. Employee owned company E provides internet solutions to a range of sectors. It does not publish a social report.

Not so easy is it? Actually three of these are private businesses and a couple are two of the best known social enterprises in the country[1]. Categorising organisations and boxing off

[1] Company A www.rsclare.com   Company B www.thebigissue.co.uk   Company C www.brighthouse.info
Company D www.diy.com   Company E www.poptel.org

some as social and others as – what, anti-social? – is not so easy when you start to examine impacts. But that is the question – what is the impact?

Real trade with real paying customers is at the heart of things.

Our concern here is for those enterprises whose primary purpose is equity, achieving a declared social or environmental benefit. We prefer the phrase "social business" to "social enterprise". It is less ambiguous and signals that real business activity – real trade with real paying customers – is at the heart of things. But in this book we use the terms to mean the same thing.

Social enterprise = (social improvement and verification) + (competition and innovation).

People who come on Cat's Pyjamas events find the concept of the triple bottom line a helpful way of making sense of striving for more than simply financial profit or shareholder value. In reducing inequality, the social business aims to achieve positive returns on each bottom line – financial, social and environmental. Most private companies only manage the first of these though they impact on the others. The challenge for the social business is to be "profitable" on all three and at the same time. Not easy, but when it works, the three forms of profit feed each other, the increased financial profitability enabling the scale and quality of social and environmental improvements to increase. Innovation and diversification are natural by-products.

We don't have a new definition but we have come up with an equation to describe the components of a social business:

Social enterprise = (social improvement and verification) + (competition and innovation)

Social improvement and verification

Social improvement – what is the purpose of the business?

For some social enterprises this is crystal clear. The Big Issue is a news and current affairs magazine written by professional journalists and sold on the streets by homeless vendors providing them with a source of income. Reclaim[2] aims to provide real work for people with learning disabilities and mental health problems through the reclamation and sorting of waste for the recycling industry.

Create exists to provide quality training and work for people who are at a disadvantage in the labour market[3]. They repair and refurbish household appliances – fridges, cookers and washing machines, and sell them at reasonable prices providing products that people can afford.

Grameen Bank supplies micro credit to offer millions of people an escape from debt and poverty[4].

---

[2] www.shu.ac.uk/shucan/reclaim   [3] www.createuk.com   [4] www.grameen-info.org

The most successful social businesses are those with a very clear sense of purpose about how their goods and services reduce inequality. They know what they intend to do and they keep that intention under review.

Landlife works for a better environment by creating new opportunities for wildflowers and wildlife and encouraging people to enjoy them. The Chief Executive, Grant Luscombe, manages a complex structure involving three organisations including a seed production and retailing business[5]. He puts it well: "To maintain the triple bottom line, everyone involved needs constant reminding of what the group is here for. But it is a fragile thing that we don't always get right. Sharing experiences (good and bad) and learning from others helps refine the light touch needed to deliver such a precious cargo."

Be clear if you are setting up a social business that you know what and who you are for.

So, be clear if you are setting up a social business that you know what and who you are for. Lack of clarity and any ambiguity will come back to bite you later, especially when the going gets tough.

The FRC Group (FRC) claims 'we do good things, promoting equality and creating jobs for people who really need them'[6]. Its furnishing and removals business, Furniture Resource Centre, provides goods and services to thousands of people throughout the country. Its furniture retail venture, Revive, supports hundreds of low income families in Merseyside

---

[5] www.nwc.org.uk   [6] www.frcgroup.co.uk

every month and Bulky Bob's, a waste management and recycling business, collects from 60,000 homes a year. It also has a PartnerShop franchise deal with Ben & Jerry's, the ice cream company.

FRC's leadership was invited to give some advice to a social enterprise that was in danger of going out of business. It is in retail, perhaps the hardest way to earn a social enterprise living. It had a fantastic location in a major city centre. The store itself is spacious and well appointed. The staff were passionate and committed. And yet it was haemorrhaging money. The manager was asked what the company was for. He gave a long story about fair trade, supporting volunteers, co-operative principles, and staff development, and educating school children about the injustice of the world's trading system – oh, and selling things to customers! They had forgotten their primary purpose and allowed other stuff – all in its way laudable – to become attached and thus pull it away from its core mission of selling products to people so that Third World suppliers could make a fair living.

The window of the store summed up the confusion of purpose and is a handy metaphor for the problems we all have in trying to cope with a wide range of people and interests. On a large curtain, which obscured the actual inside of the shop, there were posters for lots of very good causes, and some of the more exotic products, but nothing with a price on. Passers by would never know if it were a library, a community centre, or an art gallery. They certainly would never have known it was a shop that wanted to sell them things. By creating this confusion of purpose the company put its very survival at risk.

So, you're clear about your social purpose but how will you know that you are achieving it? Good intentions are fine and noble but who is to say that you are really achieving them? How can we know that the labour market interventions made by this social enterprise are cost effective and really are offering ways back in for the long term unemployed? Employing unemployed people is not enough. Many private businesses hire unemployed people. What's different about who you take on and what you do with them?

How would we know that your social business leisure services are any better in terms of social impact than the private provider down the road or the council run place across town?

You say your social enterprise is owned and managed by people who live in the neighbourhood and this has a beneficial impact in the life of your community. Really? How would you know that?

*"Oh, we haven't got any audited social accounts —
but trust us, we are doing what we claim we are doing."*

Answering these questions means measuring your achievements and having the results independently verified. First, you need to know if you are delivering what you say and then you need to gain trust and credibility with others.

Later in this book we go deeper into the necessity and power of social and environmental accounting and auditing. The point we are making here is that without verification the label 'social' in 'social enterprise' is meaningless. You can claim all day that what you do is socially or environmentally beneficial but without proof – real data, gathered and assessed objectively – that's all you have – claims and an intention.

Would you invest or work in a company which said "Oh, we haven't got any audited financial accounts – but trust us, we're great – we're profitable and we've enough cash"? Yet, with a few exceptions most social enterprises (and voluntary and community groups) are effectively saying to their stakeholders (and the tax payer who provides subsidies through grants and tax and business rates exemptions): "Oh, we haven't got any audited social accounts – but trust us, we are doing what we claim we are doing".

Beneath every definition is a political stance, an ideological assumption. Hands up. Ours is the moral imperative to be accountable to stakeholders and customers. Accountability and the willingness to be independently scrutinised are the acid tests of the social business.

We would like to see every organisation publishing an audited social report but for a social business this is fundamental.

Accountability and the willingness to be independently scrutinised are the acid tests of the social business.

Competition and innovation

Being enterprising means competing for customers and revenue in open markets and creating new products and services which address the social purpose.

With some social businesses real competition is an ever present reality.

Shoppers could choose to go to Revive or they could spend their money somewhere else (and for a couple of loss making years they did just that!). You can spend your money buying a Big Issue or you can put that pound towards a copy of Hello! ECT Recycling operates kerbside recycling contracts for local authorities, innovative recycling schemes and commercial recycling[7]. The business has to go head to head with large private waste companies every time it bids for work. Real competition, real business activity with a social hit.

The Eldonians was set up as a housing co-operative in the late 1970s in order to oppose the redevelopment of the estates around Eldon Street and Burlington Street in the Vauxhall area of Liverpool[8]. It has become one of the most successful models of community regeneration, providing not only new homes through the community-based housing association which emerged from the co-op, but also a community development trust working with local businesses and companies to invest in employment in their area.

Says Lol Santangelli, Eldonians Chief Executive: "As social enterprises we must obliterate our reliance on long term grant dependency. This is achieved by thoroughly market testing new ideas, commercial attitudes and the delivery of the very best quality services. This is an

[7] www.ectrecycling.co.uk   [8] www.eldonians.org.uk

attitude which we must adhere to in order to secure our long term survival and to make sure our social impacts are maximised".

If the customer is king that means others are not. The staff. The board. They are important but not the top dog. Many organisations can lose sight of this and get bogged down in internal issues. And the further you get from your customer the more difficult this becomes. The organisation has become the end not the means to the end. In competitive markets with real customers who can choose to buy elsewhere, the organisation is the means to the end – happy customers. Most community groups and voluntary organisations are not exposed to the impact of customers who can switch their purchasing from one day to the next.

Focusing on competition gets around the problem that arises if you use earned income as a measure of enterprising activity. This was fine until grants from local authorities were argued to be earned income. Well, perhaps, but let's not spend too much time on the fascinating game *What's My Grant?*

If the money is won competitively – that is, all companies can have a go – including private businesses – and a profit can be made on the contract – then yes, that's earning income.

For the same level of profit, there is less risk in lots of small contracts than one big one.

It is sometimes claimed that an organisation will be more sustainable (i.e. live longer) if it moves away from grants and over to earned income. We think this misses the point. If you

Can we please agree to stop using the terms "non-profit" and "not for profit"?

are managing a business, you will become more sustainable if you increase the numbers of customers. For the same level of profit, there is less risk in lots of small contracts than one big one. Diversification into other sources of income is good business and the big opportunities are in competitively won contracts.

If you are successfully enterprising you will make money. After all your costs have been met, there's cash left over. Profits. Debate has raged around the use of profits but it is premature given the small number of social businesses making profits in Britain today! Getting worked up about the ultimate destination of profit which, in most companies, will be under 10% – probably less than 5% – of income is not a good use of your time. Much better to spend that energy ensuring that the other 90% plus is spent in a way that supports and does not conflict with your objectives.

And on the subject of profit, can we please agree to stop using the terms "non-profit" and "not for profit"? Not only do they use a negative to define our businesses, they signal a distaste for making money and create confusion, particularly with our private partners. Moreover, there is the danger that some will see "not for profit" as a set of instructions rather than a constitutional form!

There remains strong ideological resistance within the voluntary and community sectors to the very idea of the market let alone the making of profits. "Some of us have mental blocks," Peruvian social entrepreneur Juan Infante says. "We are reluctant to deal with market issues. The '60s and '70s are still present in our minds. We need to acknowledge that these are skills that we need to develop, otherwise we aren't going to be able to develop our organisations, nor develop the enterprises of people that we want to push forward." Infante's organisation is called Necesitamos Millionarios (We need Millionaires)!

There is a reason for wanting to make a decent profit. Without profit you can't do the fourth important element of social business – innovate. Social businesses often provide services in markets where private businesses and the public sector have not been able to deal adequately with injustices such as homelessness and long term unemployment. In other words, two other groups of people – those looking to make money for themselves or their shareholders and those with a public duty to provide services – have failed to come up with big enough answers.

The social business sees an opportunity in that gap.

So, it must follow that the need for innovation must be a precondition because 'business as usual' has not worked. However, our impression is that in the social economy sector, innovation is treated as a nice add on if and when there is time and money (and energy) to

Finding answers to problems where others have failed demands innovation. No innovation – no social business.

do it. It can, in other words be left to one side; it's a bit of a luxury. We take the opposite view. Finding answers to problems where others have failed demands innovation. No innovation – no social business.

It is the new orthodoxy in government circles, think tanks, the regeneration industry and its media, that social enterprises are a good thing. More specifically that social enterprises which can find markets in which to trade and so achieve their social objectives and earn the cash they need to keep going, are a great thing. Around the nation there are some shining examples which are held up time and again as best practice. The clear success of the FRC's, Big Issues and Coin Street Builders[9] of the world can sometimes be praised in ways which are a rebuke to other voluntary and community activity which has failed to become profitable and which requires ongoing subsidy and tax payers' intervention.

Let's be clear. There are many grant funded organisations throughout the country doing great work in poor communities. As long as they can verify the value of their impact then good luck to them. There is nothing wrong with tax payers' or donors' money being used to keep open services to excluded people who otherwise would go without or to subsidise recycling in low income communities.

Developing earned income through sales in open markets is not and should never be compulsory.

[9] www.coinstreet.org

The truth is that the majority of social enterprises will have started with a small number of customers and probably received a grant. And the ratio of earned income to grants is unlikely to remain static over time. "Grants" and "subsidy" are not dirty words and many businesses in the private sector receive a range of subsidies, just as do community and voluntary organisations. Many European governments provide financial assistance to businesses, to such an extent that European legislation on State Aid continues to be a hot topic.

Perhaps we should replace the word "subsidy" with "compensation". Tony Rowan, Head of Finance for the FRC Group says: "We're prepared to – we exist to – take on people the private sector can't or won't touch. That brings extra costs. I don't see it as subsidy – that implies unfair advantages. The word is compensation. We take on extra management burdens and we get compensated by the tax payer. A fair deal".

Developing earned income through sales in open markets is not and should never be compulsory. We have never argued that all voluntary and community activity should be pushed kicking and screaming into the market there to live or die in some kind of social enterprise Darwinian natural selection. At our Cat's Pyjamas events, we challenge people to think very hard about whether they have got what it takes to reconfigure their organisations to be able to trade. Some people leave our events clear that they will not be able to move into competitive markets. And that is fine; they have probably avoided a future of troubled sleep and organisational pain!

Being business like and being a business
are not the same things.

And so the question is: should voluntary and community organisations commit themselves to the risky and often painful transformation process required to earn income through the sales of products and services in competitive markets?

Our answer is: "no, don't do it. Go back and think again".

There will always be public money available to fund good work in poor communities. City Challenge was followed by Single Regeneration Budget, and then came the New Deal for Communities and the Neighbourhood Renewal Fund and so on and on. It may be getting more difficult to get hold of and the paperwork may be a nightmare. But good work will always get cash. The state will always need local agencies to spend tax payers' money in order to alleviate poverty or build up local capacity. Neither do we underestimate the considerable challenges of holding on to that funding. This doesn't mean that organisations, charities, development trusts, tenants associations or whatever cannot become more business like in their activities – better at controlling costs and quicker at getting projects to deliver. But being business like and being a business are not the same things.

You need to be clear about your purpose and values,
business savvy, obsessively passionate, hard as nails,
ideologically promiscuous, shameless and very lucky.

But, if you're still with us, and you are sick and tired of the yearly fundraising slog and the mountain of paperwork you have to fill in to placate The Funder, (although you accept the need for controls in the way that tax payers' money is spent) then read on. And if you hear about one more government scheme, initiative, zone, new deal or pathfinder, you will start losing the will to live – stay with us! You will need to be ambitious and serious about wanting to make a difference.

You want to be freed from the tyranny of grant money, from the agendas of funders and donors. You want the headroom which profitability brings you, to innovate, diversify and take more risks, to achieve more of your social purpose. Great. Let's move on to some of the big issues you'll need to get your head round, whatever the form your social enterprise takes – community owned, co-op, charitable trading subsidiary, development trust.

To run a profitable social business you need to be clear about your purpose and values, business savvy, obsessively passionate, hard as nails, ideologically promiscuous, shameless and very lucky.

Sound like you?

Read on!

Boundaries
to business?
of legal structure and
red herrings

"The best ideas are common property."

Seneca

A ccording to one school of thought, some of the businesses we have cited in this book are not social enterprises at all because there is no control over them by the "community".

For some, the only genuine social enterprise is the community enterprise defined by its geographical location and the control exercised over it by the people (or some of the people) who live there. John Pearce, a director of Community Business Scotland Network, in his book *Social Enterprise in Anytown*[1] argues passionately for a very tight and excluding definition. For him, the "principle of common ownership should be reaffirmed as a non-negotiable defining characteristic". Indeed social enterprise, he asserts, is not about business, but is a "practical manifestation of an altogether bigger project, namely, changing the way society is run". The social enterprise is an end in itself, the experience of democratic ownership at least as important as the products and services for its customers.

For others, the co-operative principle is the most evolved form of social enterprise life. The co-op movement employs thousands of people in a range of markets, from cradle to grave, and is worth billions of pounds. Advocates of the co-op argue that they are the mother of all social enterprises.

The belief that one form of organisation is in itself inherently more socially good is an ideological construct. From the perspective of the customer, the quality and verifiability of the service and product are more important than the legal structure of the delivery organisation. Does it matter to the householder if domestic waste is recycled by a locally owned small or medium sized enterprise (SME) or a local co-operative? Will the good

[1] www.cbs-network.org.uk   John's book is available at www.centralbooks.co.uk

From the perspective of the customer the quality and verifiability of the service and product is more important than the legal structure of the organisation.

intentions of the chair of the development trust which runs the day care centre, matter one jot to you as you look for an affordable and safe place for your child? Does the fact that this furniture retail unit does not distribute its profits make it less or more likely I'll buy a sofa there? Or is it irrelevant?

We're with the Scottish Executive on this[2]: "As in the public and private sectors, some organisations in the social economy are well run and some badly run, some are open to new methods and some are not".

What makes the difference to any organisation are not the constitution or memoranda and articles of association but the people involved and how well they understand their markets and the need to grow and innovate. You know – entrepreneurial spirit and determination.

Does ownership effect results?

Is ownership important? Of course it is. Is the way income and wealth are distributed in our society a cause of concern? Of course. But social businesses are not political parties. They are

[2] www.scotland.gov.uk

businesses and need to focus on this as much as their future vision of society if they are to survive. It's hard enough managing a double bottom line without trying to change property rights at the same time.

The legal structure issue as part of a definition of social business is a red herring.

If the social enterprise represents one way of increasing local empowerment then structures with a higher degree of local ownership should be seen as the purpose of the business rather than necessarily having to be its defining organising principle.

We think the legal structure issue as part of a definition of social business is a red herring. Choose the legal structure that will be most effective in achieving your social objectives. For some, this will mean some form of community ownership, for others it won't. Either way you should still be accountable to all the people and organisations which matter to your business.

Do particular forms of legal structure make for better businesses? Is there credible data to demonstrate a consistent link between ownership and effectiveness in terms of outcomes? We can't find it.

For example, the London Social Economy Taskforce[3] claims that the social enterprise model has benefits over the small private firm but does so without producing any hard evidence. Its claims are anecdotal and aspirational. As a difference to private businesses, social enterprises are, 'able to build community loyalty and maintain support through difficult times'. Maybe. But

[3] 'A Social Enterprise Business Support Strategy for London - Time to Deliver' www.sel.org.uk

Claims about the merits of social enterprise are too often based upon ideology, aspirations, emotions and anecdotal evidence.

what about the post office and corner shop in rural communities? They are not social enterprises and yet manage to build lots of trust and loyalty in difficult times. At the other end of the spectrum, Apple Computers (with a very different sort of community) was able to build considerable trust and loyalty when the going got tough.

Co-operatives UK helpfully provided us with many press articles about inspiring examples of co-operative action across Europe[4]. But we could not find data to determine that co-op or other forms of ownership are systematically "better" – more profitable, longer lasting, more innovative, better for employees – than any other form. It depends – on size, sector and people.

The truth is that this is an unanswerable question. There are just too many variables. To organise a controlled study would require finding a social enterprise or co-op in the same area as an SME, doing the same things over the same timescale. And even if it was theoretically possible, who is going to pay for it?

This is not to make anyone wrong. We are agnostic about forms of ownership and their relative merits. But we need to be honest. The claims about the merits of social enterprise – however you define it – are too often based upon ideology, aspirations, emotions and anecdotal evidence. All fine but no basis on which to make an analysis.

[4] www.cooperatives-uk.coop

Not all social businesses are community owned and, using our intention-verification-competition-innovation template, we would say that not all community owned enterprises are social businesses.

When is this important?

Let's look at the honestly held beliefs that "local ownership" is necessary.

In a globalised economy dominated by vast, distant corporations willing to move capital around to the most "flexible" labour market, it is understandable that people – especially those who have experienced factory closures dumping whole communities on to the dole – will want to feel they are in control.

Advocates of the primacy of the community enterprise model argue that local ownership ensures that the business meets local needs, that profit remains in the local community and that the business won't move away when things get hard. These are entirely noble and worthwhile aspirations. Indeed, much of the UK Government's neighbourhood renewal strategy is based upon the assumption that the social enterprise must be owned and run by local people. Two strategies become intertwined – increasing enterprise and employment with experiments in local democracy.

But there are some really tough issues to face in trying to create and sustain a self sufficient business that is restricted to a small, geographically defined and deprived neighbourhood.

If you do choose the community ownership model there are some questions that you will need to address in reporting to your stakeholders.

If you are a membership organisation, how many of your local community are members? At what point can you honestly say you speak for the community rather than just representing the views of your community organisation – 70% of residents as members? 80%? 100%?

How do you deal with the voice of those who do not want to be members but are affected by, and want changes to, your services? How do you select and deselect the board? How do you make sure that the board does not use the local ownership card to trump complaints about quality and customer service? And what about that other organisation half a mile away claiming local ownership and delivering similar services?

The experience of the Eldonians in north Liverpool is essential learning for all community based enterprises. A highly successful group, they have brought about amazing transformations within their community, including the building and running of a housing estate in one of Europe's poorest neighbourhoods. The big challenge for them now is how they literally grow beyond the fence around the estate. After a lot of debate and soul searching, they have opted for an expansion strategy called 'Beyond the Boundaries'. "We simply have to find and exploit new markets to generate new income to sustain ourselves into the future," asserts Chief Executive Lol Santangelli, "we must develop the Eldonian 'brand' or it will stagnate. Staying put behind the fence is not for us a realistic option."

*It's like judging a striker by the boots he wears
rather than the number of goals he's scoring.*

They are developing products and services to sell to people far beyond the community from which they emerged. Does this mean that customers in these new areas should now share in the ownership? If so, how? And what happens if the Eldonians want to carry out developments on the territory of another community based enterprise claiming the neighbourhood representation mandate? Whose interests should come out on top?

But, let's say, unlike the Eldonians, you decide not to grow in order to avoid these issues and remain an organisation raising income from and delivering services to your very local community. Well, you will probably need an ongoing source of public funding and you will probably have to deliver a wide range of services to generate a viable business model. The wider the range of products and services, the harder the management issues.

If you choose not to use a community ownership model, but your objectives are to deliver benefits to local communities, then you will need to be clear on how you listen to and respond to them.

Whichever, way you go – co-op, development trust, whatever – running any business is hard. Prioritising local ownership will make it harder, and balancing the aspiration of local control with real world business realities can add complexity and costs. There are no easy solutions to any of this. But it is critical for you to go into the community owned enterprise model with eyes wide open. Putting community ownership – however defined – as the cornerstone of the business has many and varied consequences which will, at the very least, restrict future options for developing the business.

The general acceptance – however grudging in some parts – of the DTI's all things to all people definition of what a social enterprise is[5], has taken some of the steam out of the debate. But arguments like 'you're not a real social enterprise because half your board doesn't live within a mile of the business' miss the point. It's like judging a striker by the boots he wears rather than the number of goals he's scoring.

There has been a great deal of debate about possible new legal company forms to support the development of social enterprise[6]. In the end, for us the issue is not about legal structure. It's about accountability. Accountability to all those with whom you have a relationship, whose lives you affect or hope to affect. Remember, social enterprise is a state of mind and it is to be found in organisations of all shapes and sizes.

[5] The DTI's definition, arrived at after much negotiation and horse trading is: Social enterprises are businesses with primarily social objectives whose surpluses are principally reinvested for that purpose in the business or in the community, rather than being driven by the need to maximise profit for shareholders and owners.

[6] Such as the proposed Community Interest Company see www.dti.gov.uk/cics/

Social business leadership

surviving the social entrepreneur

*"The Philosophers have only interpreted the world:
the thing, however, is to change it."*

Karl Marx

T hink of a social business. Chances are, for good or ill, it is associated in your mind with an individual, the founder or current leader. You probably know of John Bird at the Big Issue and perhaps Tim Smit at Eden Project[1]. You may also know Tony McGann at the Eldonians, and Claire Dove at Blackburne House[2]. Internationally, can you name anyone else at Grameen Bank other than Muhammad Yunus?

It is a commonplace in business that the quality of leadership is critical and that enterprises need different sorts of leadership and management at different times in their history. For social enterprises, this is just as important, perhaps more so. To invent, sustain and grow a social business requires all the talents and insights of the private business woman or man – financial control, human resource management, customer focus and product development. But it also demands commitment to addressing the social goals of the enterprise.

The social business entrepreneur must make money and achieve social return simultaneously. On top of this come the higher expectations – sometimes unrealistic – of how the social enterprise "should" be. Employees, board, funders, customers, local residents, regeneration policy makers and politicians – all will have a view about what a "proper" social business should do or not do. The social business will usually have a range of external relationships to manage which are more extensive and complex than would be usual for a small private business. Not an easy task and not for the faint of heart.

[1] www.edenproject.org.uk   [2] www.blackburnehouse.co.uk

The social business entrepreneur must make money
and achieve social return simultaneously.

Power and Glory

The rise and rise of the social entrepreneur in recent years has been dramatic although there is no universally shared understanding or definition about what the term 'social entrepreneur' means. That's okay. A rigid definition won't add any value to anyone.

There are growing numbers of people all over the world who feel comfortable with the label "social entrepreneur" and who are creating all kinds of economic, social and environmental value. What does increasingly unite this diverse group of people is a hunger to network and learn from each other. They don't quite fit into the traditional voluntary, NGO, public or private sectors, but occupy the space where these sectors overlap, drawing the best from each and trying to create something new.

A recent international on line discussion[3] brought together hundreds of social entrepreneurs from every continent to consider definitions and impacts. Some contributors focused on the word 'entrepreneur' in the sense of the individual who runs a business. For them, a social entrepreneur runs businesses which generate revenues and profit while simultaneously pursuing a social return. Others focused on the qualities of social entrepreneurship, especially creativity and innovation. There were also much wider definitions embracing all agents of social change, whether or not they used

[3] www.socialedge.org

income-generating strategies. Muhammad Yunus offered the broadest definition: "Anybody who is offering their time to address a social or economic problem is a social entrepreneur."

Certainly not every social entrpreneur is cut out to lead and manage a social business. "One cannot assume," observes Mark Swilling founder of South Africa's inspirational Sustainability Institute, "that social entrepreneurs will make good managers of social enterprises. Many come from donor funded NGO's, and therefore have little appreciation of the notion of risk and reward."[4]

We're with Jerr Boschee, the Executive Director of the Institute for Social Entrepreneurs in Minnesota. We like his definition, it's short and to the point: "An individual who uses earned income strategies to pursue social objectives, seeking both a financial and social return on investment."[5]

Money, political patronage, awards, and media coverage are flowing towards the social entrepreneur. It is now possible to travel the world practically full time, speaking at conferences and seminars, picking up prizes and fees as part of the celebrity social entrepreneur circuit. There is, inevitably, no shortage of ego and ambition around this circuit and there are plenty of strongly held differences of opinion.

Klaus Schwab, no less, founder and director of the World Economic Forum[6], the gathering of the world's rich and powerful held every year in Davos, is a keen advocate of the social entrepreneur.

[4] www.spierinstitute.org   [5] www.socialent.org   [6] www.weforum.org

Through his foundation, Schwab wants

"to encourage and foster entrepreneurs working for the public interest – to support them and provide them with access and funding to an international platform for experience exchange that they might otherwise lack. We wanted to create a mechanism that works from the bottom up."[7]

For Schwab in Geneva, social entrepreneurs are pioneers of pattern-breaking approaches to resolve seemingly intractable problems and are mostly to be found amongst well educated middles class professionals. London's School for Social Entrepreneurs would give this analysis the shortest of shrifts!

Schwab has made the amazing work of some social entrepreneurs better known. People such as Vijay Mahajan of Basix, a company which promotes sustainable livelihoods through financial services and technical assistance[8]. Or Roy Stear of Freeplay, a company which seeks to create and develop the market for self sufficient energy products whilst balancing the imperatives of both profit and social justice[9]. Getting people like Rick Aubry of San Francisco's Rubicon Enterprises past the security cordons to debate issues of economic justice with the big hitters from business is not something we'd want to prevent[10].

Seriously rich guy Jeff Skoll, the creator of eBay, through his foundation is also championing social entrepreneurs, and through Social Edge, doing a great job sustaining a virtual ideas marketplace where entrepreneurs from every corner of the globe can connect and learn from one another.

[7] www.schwabfound.org   [8] www.basixindia.com   [9] www.freeplaygroup.com   [10] www.rubiconpgms.org

However, the social entrepreneur model has its limitations and dangers. It's true that good ideas come from enterprising individuals with the passion and drive to make things happen and bring other people and communities with them. But the focus on the glorious individual can obscure the collective effort that is required to make success possible. Big business and political elites have no problem with letting in the charismatic and successful individual to tell them about poverty and how bad it is. They are not so keen on mass movements challenging their power. They tend to get tear-gassed, not offered cocktails. It will be interesting to see how Schwab deals with the World Social Forum which is coming from a very different ideological space.[11]

The focus on the socially entrepreneurial leader can distract from the brute political realities that many of our communities' ills need far reaching structural changes in the way our state works. It is one thing for the corporate masters of the universe who meet at the WEF to applaud the inspirational social entrepreneurs in Bangladesh, Cameroon and Bolivia. Quite another for them to do something about the grotesque inequalities of the world's trading system – subsidy and protection for European and North American businesses and ruthless free market globalism for everyone else.

A million social business entrepreneurs can show how things can be done in radically different ways but they cannot redistribute wealth or compel large businesses to take responsibility for the mess they make. Systemic change requires government action or, in other words, that we as a people decide that we no will no longer accept that children will die of malnutrition, that millions are homeless or that the gap between the haves and have nots gets wider.

[11] www.wsfindia.org

Should they stay or should they go?

For those social entrepreneurs who do go on to lead and manage a social business, one big issue raised with us again and again is leadership exit strategy or, more often, the lack of it.

The departure of the founder is a real moment of truth. Is the management and financial control robust enough to survive his or her departure? Often, inspirational founding entrepreneurs neither like nor are good at the myriad tasks which fall into the Dull But Vitally Important category. Problems get solved not by having systems in place to manage them but by the leader's heroic intervention. Or, as one disgruntled employee in a well known social business put it: "He thrives on problems. Leaves it until the last minute and then pulls another rabbit out of the hat. It's like Watership Down here sometimes. It's wearing."

And when the heroes leave, the holes which have been filled or hidden by their energy and unchallengeable authority, become all too evident. In one example, the Inspirational Founder's successor found that when she tried to pull the levers of power they weren't connected to anything. There were no systems, records, protocols – nearly everything had been run on the basis of the founder's say so.

The Inspirational Founder with unshakeable self belief, the 'with me or against me' drive, the innate deal making capability, the 'my word is my bond' business style can produce marvellous results at start up stage and beyond. Those traits that can be problematic later on are just what's needed at the beginning. "This is my vision, join me or get out of the way." Just what's required to overcome all the barriers that will be thrown in the way.

But later, as the enterprise matures, this style of leadership can become increasingly damaging. It's tantamount to treating everyone as children if the ability to succeed is based on winning the attention and patronage of the leader. The company *is* the founder in the eyes of everyone and there is no headroom for others to grow. Everyone else has walk on parts in the founder's drama and that is ultimately demotivating and undermining.

> *Those traits that can be problematic later on are just what's needed at the beginning.*

This is not, of course, always the case. Happy the social business and rare are those founders who consciously decide to move on before they start damaging their creation. It is a very difficult thing to pull off. This is their baby in whom they have invested years of their lives and a great deal of emotion. Nic Frances, who founded FRC, is one such social entrepreneur who successfully managed his exit, passing on the torch without the flame being extinguished or too many people getting burned.

Anne McNamara, the co-founder of The Big Issue in the North, also left well after nearly 10 years. Anne realised early on that long term survival would be based on creating a socially entrepreneurial culture in which innovation and creativity were not the preserve of the leader but were everyone's focus and responsibility.

It can be very difficult to exert an appropriate level of management over the chief executive, still less show them the door when past their use by date.

She makes the important point that one of the problems with social enterprises is that it is not easy to provide a financial exit to the founders who may have invested years, energy, youth and a lot of their own money in the social enterprise. People can stay, not because they are still adding value, but because they have invested so much and are unable to extract the value. In many cases, the legal structure is not the barrier, it is the fact that financial exits have not been used and are deemed to be unethical. But, what is more unethical, asks Anne, founders hanging around on big salaries for years after they have lost the love for their organisation or a financial settlement which means they and the business can move on?

The founder often appoints the board, can be appointed the chief executive or decide to be chief executive but can be impossible to remove if he or she is the majority shareholder or member. If the company is not a charity where the power rests with the trustees, it can mean that the founder never becomes accountable to anybody.

So why should founders leave? In private businesses there is no compulsion on the owner to move on so why should there be in social enterprise? In part, the answer is that there is a wider group of people to whom the founder is answerable, of which directors are one group and the people who are benefiting from the activities of the business are another. In the private sector, external shareholders do exert influence over founders' roles and responsibilities especially as the business grows. And this is the point, if the objective is growth, it may well be the case that the time comes for the Inspirational Founder to move on, however effective they have been with a smaller organisation. Everyone has an optimum time with an organisation. That is the spirit of enterprise – change, growth, and development.

The business has become the monument to the founder not a dynamic idea being shaped by life's possibilities.

As potentially damaging as the departing founder who leaves a mess, is the founder who leaves and keeps interfering. This is a particularly acute issue in neighbourhood based community enterprises where the founder lives, literally, next door to the business. This is his idea. His building. He who fought the naysayers and politicians to get all this built. That vision can become limiting, excluding even the consideration of different futures. The business has become the monument to the founder not a dynamic idea being shaped by life's possibilities.

How depressing it is to visit the social enterprise shaped and trapped by the 'seen-it-all' founder leader, second guessing the chief executive and acting as brake on new ideas. The move from leader to elder is not easy to do well.

An issue we are trying to address through the Cat's Pyjamas is that of on-going formation and support for social enterprise leaders. It is important not to over emphasise the differences between the leadership of private companies and that of social business. But

Passionate about their enterprises and the social and environmental purposes, they tend to be ideologically and sectorally promiscuous.

there are unique challenges for social business leaders and there are few sources of credible leadership development support available.

We have noticed that there are some common characteristics amongst the leaders of successful social enterprises which suggest areas in which support could be more systematic in the future. They are restlessly driven and ruthless in pursuing their objectives. Whilst passionate about their enterprises and the social and environmental purposes, they tend to be ideologically and sectorally promiscuous. In other words they network far and wide, they seek their learning from wherever they can and are excellent at adapting what they learn into their own businesses. They are curious and very skilled at creating around themselves great teams. For those who lead large businesses, more and more of their learning is coming from the leading edge of innovation in the private sector and they are shameless shoplifters (metaphorically speaking of course!).

So, if you are trying to recruit a chief executive for your social enterprise, we suggest you look for these qualities.

Board games

necessary evil or source of support and wisdom?

"Indecision is like a stepchild: if he does not wash his hands, he is called dirty, if he does, he is wasting water. "

African Proverb

A gain and again at Cat's Pyjamas events, we hear the horror stories about weak or risk averse boards, conflict between directors and senior staff, and the poor quality of data and analysis passing between the two.

Good governance of any business is crucial and a social enterprise, attempting to create and sustain profits on two and three bottom lines, is no exception. Too often we see companies within which the board is seen as a necessary evil to be manoeuvred around every couple of months, rather than being a key part of the business's success, providing strategic direction and support to the executive team.

The board is responsible for complying with the relevant law and, with this, comes a substantial chunk of financial responsibility. However, there is little legal responsibility for the social return of the organisation's work and, unless the board does have a strong strategic role and understanding, it is possible that the traditional management information that it requests will underplay the social issues and knock the organisation off its primary purposes.

Create is a spin out from FRC, established in the mid-nineties in partnership with Thorn EMI. Whilst still in its start up period, the board of Create began a strategy of national expansion and took their eyes off the ball in the local market in Speke in south Liverpool. No-one was taking a hard look at the finances and the underlying trends. There were a lot of theoretical budgets and too many unchallenged ifs and maybes in management's planning.

Too often the board is seen as a necessary evil to be manoeuvred around every couple of months.

Create's board had members with experience of managing big business and for whom Create's budget was relatively small. It was an excellent board for getting it up and going, with lots of movers and shakers, but they were people who were too busy and geographically dispersed. They consequently relied too much on the skills of an inexperienced management team who found it hard to tell this great board that things weren't going well.

The initial emphasis, correctly for that stage of its development, was on the training of long term unemployed people. But even then training contracts were being offered to people for longer than the funding that would be available to support them. External requirements from training purchasers focused, understandably, on the training element. This meant that management reporting was funding led and not business led. A simple mistake but one which led to the brink of insolvency. The business was saved only by considerable intervention from one or two board members and with support from private and public sector allies.

In fact, Create's business model was built on retail sales for a product that would take time to be established. The market for recycled white goods is particularly dependent on building a reputation for reliability and service, a reputation that largely comes through word of mouth. But with the management information focused on the training part of the business, the board couldn't see the full picture and so take appropriate decisions and course correct.

So, make sure the objective, a social business based on sales, is clear. Make sure the business plan reflects this objective and that the management information systems monitor progress against these objectives – as well as providing the information required by others.

Time and energy must be spent on building relationships of trust between board and management.

Today, Create Liverpool is doing very well in a tight margin business. Create learned the hard way that time and energy must be spent on building relationships of trust between board and management and having clear reliable information systems which create head room for the board to focus on strategic, governance and verification issues not fire fighting.

The board of another social enterprise involved in recycling in the North West asked FRC to advise them about how they could get out of a financial hole. The chair was asked for the latest accounts and copies of the last set of papers sent to the board. This request was met with silence. It turned out that there was no agreed system for sharing information. In truth no-one really knew what was going on at all. It was clear the business was insolvent and the only course of action was to wind it up. Well so what, small firms go bust all the time? The issue here though is that this social enterprise – now closed – had received a great deal of public money and had enjoyed an easy ride in the media as just the sort of socially entrepreneurial initiative the inner cities need.

Graham Morris, a leading car industry figure, was recruited to chair the board of FRC specifically to beef it up and help close the gap between the directors and the leadership of the business. "I saw straight away," says Graham, "that the board was too often playing catch up. This was in no way because of bad blood or a desire by the executive team to deliberately mislead."

"Remember I'm not getting paid for this so I want to make a real contribution not chase dodgy figures!"

His analysis was that the quality of the information coming to board meetings was poor. "If, as a non-executive director, you feel that you can't fully trust the figures then inevitably you will end up seeking assurances at the meeting about them. This is how you wind up talking about the chief exec's mileage rather than adding real value to the company by addressing strategic business issues and holding the team to account for the social returns. Remember I'm not getting paid for this so I want to make a real contribution not chase dodgy figures!"

Time can therefore be wasted focusing on the micro. But it is equally bad practice to waste time discussing Life, the Universe and Everything or complaining about the baddies at the council or in No 10. Understanding the larger context is vital for any business but make sure you are discussing these things appropriately and using valuable board time to the maximum value for the business and social goals of the organisation.

It takes time and deliberately targeted energy to build the trust between board and staff which ensures that the territory between governance and management is a creative space and not a battlefield. Agree with your board how much information they want and when. In what formats? Who gets what? What is for discussion and what simply for information? FRC use videos to help keep the board informed. In a rapidly growing and diversifying social business it can be tough to keep the board up to speed, not only with the facts, but the feel and culture of the place. Videos featuring staff, customers, and other stakeholders reflect the business back to the board so they know what's going on and what influences are shaping the thinking of the leadership team. Technology is making this kind of creativity more and more accessible.

As trust grows, the amount of paperwork should decrease. "The amount of papers being sent to the board in advance of meetings is inversely proportional to the trust which exists between them" says Graham Morris. "Distrustful boards demand more paperwork."

The social accounting process is a big help in ensuring that board/senior management relationships are productive. The process begins with the board agreeing what its social objectives are and then analysing the data which helps it determine whether or not it is achieving them. This should make everyone clear about why they are there and why they focus on some issues and not others. We return to this in a later chapter.

The community based enterprise has an added challenge if the board must be drawn from local residents because the pool of talent to draw on is necessarily more limited. Where will the new insights and energy at board level come from? It is vital to have a regular turnover of people at board level. How will stagnation be avoided if there are simply not enough people locally willing or able to stand? And how will you prevent the legitimate concern for local issues – "what about my community?" – becoming a paralysing parochialism preventing growth and diversification – "*nowhere* but my community"? This is an issue which we hear about over and over again from the social enterprises we meet all over the country.

Many social enterprises have no strategy for recruiting board members. And it is often too easy to get elected. It is no easy job to find high quality board members. There is no financial reward available and we would argue that this will need to change if social business becomes big business. And the time may come when paid executive directors will be the only way to close the gap between board and management leadership. Whilst it's dangerous to recruit board members before you know what skills you are looking for, everyone involved will have personal and business contacts. Get on the phone and use them. If you really don't have any, join some organisations like your local Chamber of Commerce[1] and get your networks buzzing for you.

There is one question which we get asked at every event we run. What do you do with a board that doesn't want to change or blocks innovation either through inertia or ideological hostility?

Truth is, you have to be honest with yourself and with the board. Without common purpose between management leadership and the board nothing much of value can be achieved. There is no choice but to be straight with the board members. If they do not share your passion and vision, well, maybe it is time to move on. Focus on the potential increased financial viability and increased social mission which can be achieved through social business.

[1] www.britishchambers.org.uk

Without common purpose between management leadership and board nothing much of value can be achieved.

Encourage them to get out and meet the boards of social businesses which have begun the journey. Get them at a Cat's Pyjamas event. Inspiration guaranteed! There is nothing like seeing in order to believe.

But as we have said before social business is not – and should not be – for everyone. Sometimes culture change is like trying to put lipstick on a bulldog! It's exhausting work, it doesn't look right and even if you can get the lipstick on, it's still a bulldog!

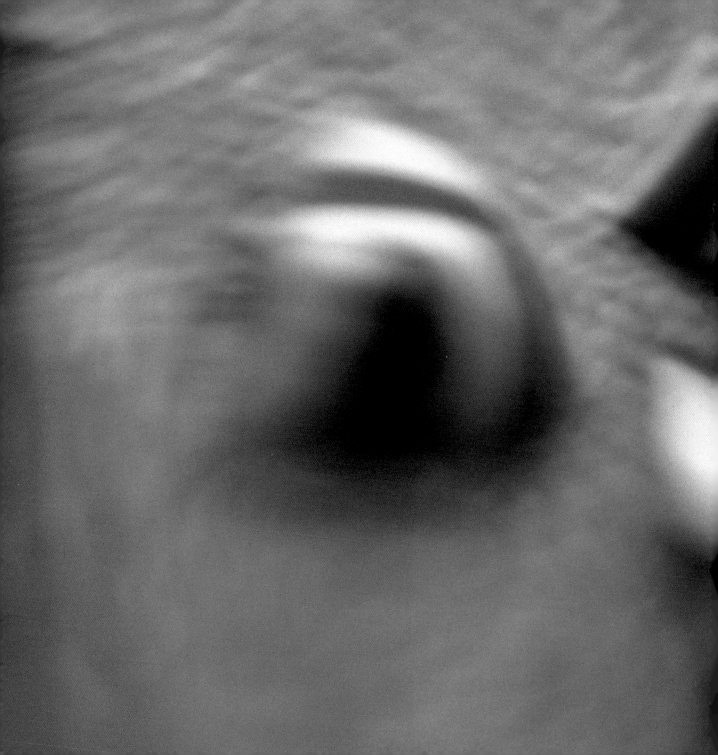

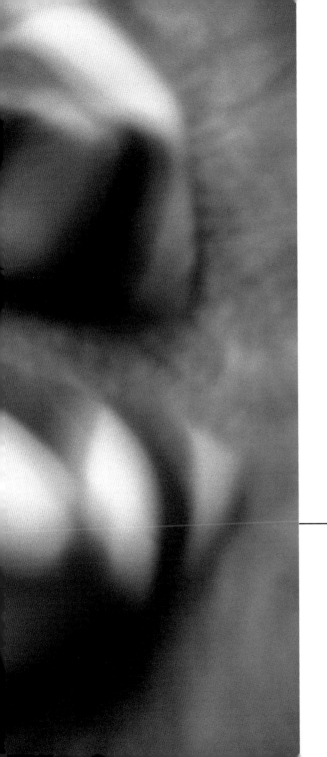

Juggling underwater

managing a triple bottom line

"Do or do not. There is no try."

Yoda, Jedi Master

Y ou're the sales manager for the Big Issue magazine. You are paid to maximise sales so that you can attract more advertising revenue. Yet the resettlement programme removes your best sales people every month, replacing them with less reliable and inexperienced vendors.

Or, over in Liverpool, you're the logistics manager at FRC charged with making sure millions of pounds worth of furniture arrives on time to thousands of homes around the country. And a third of your workforce leaves every year to be replaced by people who have been selected precisely because they have been out of work for ages and do not have the skills you need!

Getting the balance right between running a business and staying focused on the social purposes is tough and causes deep angst inside social enterprises. Here we want to explore what happens when brute economics meet strongly held values. This goes to the heart of the challenge of managing the double and triple bottom line.

Done right, there really is no business like social business. Great products and services producing lovely profits on each of your bottom lines. But, sometimes running a social enterprise is like trying to juggle underwater. And finding those jugglers is no easy matter. Recruiting and retaining managers and staff who can, on a daily basis, keep both commercial reality and the social purpose in view is not easy.

But, once you enter into a real and competitive marketplace to sell your products and services, prepare to have your values and social purposes put under continuing pressure. FRC prided itself on having opened up a market for furnished tenancies in North West England. It set the standard and that standard was high quality products. Why should social housing tenants not have stuff as good as or better than can be got from IKEA or DFS? Fine. Happy tenant. Happy FRC able to stay true to its principles and make money.

How you handle such challenges to your founding principles will decide whether it's the pressure that produces diamonds or the stress that leads to breakdown.

But what's this? A private company, with no social agenda and associated costs and management challenges, copied FRC's service and offered landlords cheaper and lower quality products. FRC starts to lose market share and margins fall. Question: should it trot on to the moral high ground and hold firm to the entirely legitimate principle that just because you're poor you shouldn't be offered lesser quality and watch the competitor clean up? Or perhaps retaliate with a secondary range of cheaper products? Or, begin to withdraw from a marketplace where it has now very successfully mainstreamed the service and move on?

In fact, it got ahead of the game again by innovating and bringing to market a range of new products and services to differentiate it from its competitors. Says Shaun Doran, who runs FRC's increasingly diverse range of businesses: "It doesn't feel nice at the time, but there is no doubt we are offering our customers who have low incomes a better, more responsive service, because there is competition out there pushing back at us all the time. It removes complacency and keeps us very focused on balancing income, profit and service to the people this organisation was set up to help 15 years ago".

How you handle such head on challenges to your founding principles will decide whether it's the pressure that produces diamonds or the stress that leads to breakdown. And the truth is there will be times when you simply have to put the social purpose on the backburner and just make some bloody money to pay the wages and the rent. Such crisis driven pragmatism is inevitable, but the challenge is when and how you get back on track with your social purposes. If the bottom lines are dramatically out of synch, do you have the systems and people to get them back in balance?

As Sheffield Rebuild's turnover grew by over 1000% in 4 years, the demands of this outstripped the staff team's capacity to manage[1]. Turnover looked great but margins were poor or negative. They were fortunate because they were able to generate cash from new parts of the business that could be grown quickly and because at least one of their large clients was willing to stand by them when things were bad. But to survive, the commercial side of the business had to take precedence and there was no system for managing the scale, duration or impact of getting the social and enterprise objectives out of kilter. Rebuild came through this and was the highest placed social enterprise in the 2002 Inner City 100 list of high growth businesses in deprived urban areas and were again in the top 100 in 2003 with their social agenda at the heart of the business.

There are no easy answers to how you rebalance your social business when hit by crisis, but having a clear purpose and set of values does provide the parameters within which such judgments can be made. If external factors – changed market, brilliant new competitor –

[1] www.sheffieldrebuild.co.uk

knock you off balance and you are not clear about what your primary social purposes are, how will you know how to get back to them?

Here, again, the importance of social reporting is obvious. The very process of stating and restating your social and environmental objectives, gathering data, assessing it and having it independently verified will keep you focused on the state of your bottom lines and where changes and course corrections are required.

Through its social reporting, it became clear to FRC that a core part of its business activities was out of balance. On the face of it, there seemed nothing wrong with the furniture refurbishment programme. In truth, it was a small part of the business in terms of turnover and people employed, but iconically it was a very powerful part of the culture and what FRC felt itself to be about. Furniture was collected, refurbished by trainees and sold to low income families through Revive. Fantastic. Everyone loved it – happy, formerly unemployed people productively engaged in recycling.

But, the increasing rigour of its social accounting put the cold hard data in front of the leadership team. The programme was expensive, requiring ongoing public funding to enable FRC to pay the salaries to the trainee upholsterers. This enabled the finished products to be sold at prices which carried no labour costs. Additionally, very few people were actually moving on to work in a rapidly shrinking upholstery industry. And, it turned out, it was cheaper for FRC to make new suites (and, arguably, more environmentally friendly as well). The financial bottom line was okay but the social and environmental returns were poor. The programme was wound up, enabling the company to focus its energies more productively on parts of the social business where the bottom lines could be more profitably balanced.

When Aspire got going in Bristol in the late nineties, homeless people were involved in all aspects of the business[2]. They delivered the catalogues of fair traded goods, worked in the warehouse, packed stock, and delivered it to customers' homes. The business grows. Orders flood in. To increase efficiency and speed, it is suggested that order fulfillment be outsourced to a specialised private company. The upside is that customers will get their products quicker and with less margin for error. This means more revenue and profit for Aspire and its Third World suppliers. The downside is there will be less space for homeless people. What would you do?

> *"We have lost that 'purity' of vision that we had in the early days but I hope now we have the right balance of idealism and realism."*

Well, Paul Harrod and his team decided to outsource. Growing the business and making it financially sound were given priority. There was still work for homeless people but less so and this caused unease amongst some of Aspire's supporters. A tough call, but a typical hard choice which has to be made when stakeholders' needs collide.

Paul Harrod is candid about the challenges of balancing the social vision and hard commercial realities with the demands of growing a customer facing company: "Virtually

2 www.aspire-group.com

everyone in Aspire started with a "social" perspective. We have lost that 'purity' of vision that we had in the early days but I hope now Aspire has the right balance of idealism and realism."

Values

We say that social enterprise is a state of mind because it's about your values. These are the critically important starting point. When did your company last reflect on what it believes in? Are your values clearly articulated? Don't just assume everyone in your business believes the same things or wants the same things? If you do, we guarantee there are old values lying around polluting the atmosphere and causing confusion and misunderstanding – and underperformance.

When did your company last reflect on what it believes in and how it will be in the world?

Examine your beliefs and your mission. Is it still what you do? What you want to do? What you can do? If you answer 'no' to any one of these bin them. Free yourself, get everyone together and rewrite the script.

Your values will help when it comes to recruitment. Either you will attract people with a social or an enterprise bias in their experience and have to have someone else to manage the tensions, or you will be lucky enough to find people with experience and ability in both. Hard to find but easier if you are recruiting against a set of values.

Never forget that you will be relying on people to deliver the objectives and if they have different takes on the organisation's values it will lead to trouble. FRC has spent a lot of time and energy defining, clarifying, communicating, reviewing, communicating again its cultural values of bravery, creativity, passion and professionalism. It defines values as "beliefs in action", the sets of behaviours and attitudes which define how it wants to be and how it will engage with the world. It aspires to have these values underpin all its activities as supplier, retailer, employer, trainer, procurer, and campaigner.

Everyone employed knows that one of their values is to give customers world class customer service, achieving 10 out 10. There is no ambiguity which allows old values to breathe such as the one which held that customers can get an okay service so long as its trainees are looked after. It was only during the process of defining and clarifying what the company believed that this cultural assumption was uncovered amongst some of the longer serving staff. Customers were seen as a kind of necessary evil which had to be sold things in order to do the most important thing – employing long term unemployed people. The leadership of FRC is in no doubt that the continued success of the company is in no small part due to the clarity of purpose and intent which is framed by the values which permeate the business.

Having occasionally to put people out of work becomes understood not as a normal part of the business cycle but as a moral failure.

For many social enterprises, the juggling act is most acute when it comes to peoples' jobs. For such businesses in areas of high unemployment there is an understandable cultural commitment to protect jobs. Having occasionally to put people out of work becomes understood not as a normal part of the business cycle but as a moral failure. But for social enterprise the challenge can go beyond this.

In a fast changing market, FRC decided to stop producing its own suites. It did a deal with Dove Designs, a neighbouring social enterprise helping it expand its production to supply FRC.[3] The staffing impact was that six jobs in manufacturing were made redundant. The company tried to ensure a soft landing for everyone by offering redeployment. One of the options was a transfer into FRC's logistics team (on the same pay). But this would mean that up to half a dozen places for people from long term unemployment would be lost.

The dilemma – support exsisting staff or maintain the level of opportunities for future unemployed people?

FRC's stated social purpose is to support unemployed people. So the dilemma: support existing staff or maintain the level of opportunities for future unemployed people? What the Leadership Team found was that it did not have a specific framework for dealing with this. In the end, the decision to redeploy was made against the backdrop of FRC's values. Alison Ball is FRC's Head of People and Learning: "Every time we remodel the business we have to look at the impacts on our core mission. We are in uncharted waters but we were really helped on this production issue by the fact we had a shared values vocabulary. This at

[3] www.dovedesigns.org.uk

least gave us the words to talk amongst ourselves about balancing business realities with our founding passions".

The truth about running triple bottom line social businesses is that you won't get the balance right all the time and when you think you've got it right, something will happen to send you back to the drawing board. It is a process and the challenge is to build systems and a culture in your enterprise which can deal with the non-stop challenge of balancing the tensions inherent in the very idea of trying simultaneously to make money and bring about social and environmental change.

Real people
and their money

*finding and keeping
your customers*

*"When you stop talking, you've lost your customer.
When you turn your back, you've lost her."*

Estée Lauder

The journey from grant funded organisation to sales led social business can require a massive change in culture. It involves travelling a learning curve with a right angle in it. And becoming customer focused – really focused – is one of the biggest challenges to be faced.

Good, bad and indifferent customer service is to be found in all parts of the economy and in any company there is always the risk that the needs of customers will slip down the list of cultural priorities.

In a social enterprise environment, where the range of stakeholders will be much broader than for a private business, this risk is greater. The social enterprise – particularly the community or neighbourhood specific enterprise – will often be delivering services to people who don't have a choice in the matter and who are not paying directly, a council or other procurer is. The danger is that the quality of customer service is not as good or responsive as it should be because people can't go elsewhere.

If you don't like the new range of knickers at Mark and Sparks, you can go down the high street and check out TJ Hughes or go online and order from Next. But if you live on a satellite housing estate where the council funds the local community organisation to provide IT training, and it is mediocre or poor, where else can you go? Where will you get your low cost furniture from if the local recycler is under-resourced or just plain inefficient? Monopoly provision in whatever market or sector rarely makes for customer focused brilliance and this includes social and community enterprises.

Monopoly provision rarely makes for customer focused brilliance and this includes social and community enterprises.

Customers first, your organisation second

In voluntary and community organisations, which have grown out of years of struggle, and people are rightly proud of what they have achieved, there's the risk that the survival of the organisation is put in front of the needs of clients and customers. Of course, an organisation has to exist to be able to deliver, but the best way of surviving is to focus on clients and customers first. All else follows.

Ask yourself this: how much time is spent at your board and senior management meetings on internal stuff as opposed to your marketplace, your clients and customers? Addressing the ins and outs of local tribal community politics as opposed to product innovation and new market creation? Make sure you focus on what is really important.

Kevin Jones[1] a serial entrepreneur, with seven successful private businesses to his credit over 25 plus years, moved to the social enterprise sector two years ago. His perceptions are acute: "One thing I have learned here is that process leads and content follows, whereas in business content leads and process follows." He goes on: "In private business the value of the deal becomes clear and people get over themselves in order to realise that value in business; in non-profits, they sometimes seek consensus for so long that they never get to the deal."

[1] www.collectiveintelligence.net

You can get away with organisational navel gazing and ideological posturing for a long time in a fund raised environment because most funders don't ask hard enough questions for a long enough time. When grant funding comes from a local authority, the quality of service will be only one of the determining factors of whether the cash comes next year or not. We expect you know of organisations into which the money continues to flow regardless, it seems, of what is done with it.

Ask yourself this: how much time is spent at your board and senior management meetings on internal stuff and how much on your marketplace, your clients and customers?

But there is nowhere to hide in a sales led business when your survival is dependent on how your markets and customers react to the quality and price of your goods and services. Some of Create's customers might know and even care about its brilliant support for unemployed residents in south Liverpool. But this counts for nothing – and rightly so – when those single parents or refugees with little money to spend are trying to decide if they should buy a Create washing machine. Top of their minds will be the price, whether the appliance will work when it is switched on and not flood their kitchens and, if it breaks down, will something be done about it quickly.

John Bennett, Managing Director of Cardiff's social enterprise Pack-IT,[2] half of whose employees have Down's Syndrome, remembers well the day when the customer first reality was brought home to him: "On one of my first sales pitches I learnt a lesson. A prospective customer said our work looked promising. It was a terrible November day. I said you should

[2] www.pack-it.com

There is nowhere to hide in a sales led business when your survival is dependent on how your markets and customer base react to the quality and price of your goods and services.

employ us because we have disabled people working for us and he said 'I don't give a shit who works for you. I just want to know if you can do the job'."

In a real marketplace, the customer's needs matter more than yours. It's as simple as that. You will also get competition from private suppliers, probably more focused than you, because it is their money or shareholders' money on the line. The vast majority of private suppliers do not have all the other stuff – accountability, training unemployed people, managing unreasonable political and community expectations – to contend with. All they have to worry about is price and quality.

The Big Issue is probably the one social enterprise offer where the buy is most obviously intimately tied up in the social agenda of the supplier. People buy it because they want to help homeless people. Fairtrade chocolate[3] and coffee[4] are increasing market share. But the quality of the products on sale has come a long way since the days when the only way you could swallow them was with a big spoonful of righteous anger about poverty in the Third World.

For the social business which supports unemployed people, managing customer care levels is also tricky. Take FRC. Its vehicles, criss-crossing the country, all have formerly long term unemployed people in the cabs. The secret of its training success is that its guys are doing

---

[3] www.divinechocolate.com   [4] www.cafedirect.co.uk

Competing in real markets requires a speed of decision making and risk taking which is not the hallmark of our sector.

real work with real customers and so giving them the best preparation for the logistics industry. But this means that FRC is continually putting inexperienced staff in front of customers and risking its most important asset – its reputation. Managing this requires extra time and effort – time and effort not being targeted on customers. And while FRC is doing this, its privately owned competitors are trying to steal those customers.

Risky business

Competing in real markets also requires a speed of decision making and risk taking which is not the hallmark of our sector. You will be required to take risks, and yet boards of development trusts, charities or other voluntary or community organisations are often very risk averse. This is not a criticism. Trustees are supposed to be risk averse. And if you were potentially liable for an organisation's actions but had no executive power so would you be. To some extent this is a good thing. There are resources and reputations to be safeguarded, but the result can be a culture that shies away from new ventures until success can be guaranteed. But the truth is, no business venture is guaranteed, and there is a massive casualty rate amongst new business start-ups.

Most private businesses don't seek out risk, they manage it. Social entrepreneurs are stuck into high risk ventures in areas from which most private business men and women have run a mile. Good social businesses understand and can manage the specific risks. But it is undoubtedly true that there is a conservatism in many voluntary and community based organisations which does not sit well with the speed of change which happens once you put your toe into real markets.

The indirect customer

Most social enterprises are selling small numbers of services to small numbers of customers. Most are in public sector markets and have a portfolio of long term contracts. This can create unintended difficulties for customer satisfaction because there are two masters to please.

Take Bulky Bob's. The primary customer is Liverpool City Council[5]. It is the other name on the contract and it pays the money. The other customers are the many thousands of individuals who use the service. There is obviously an overlap between the two. The Council wants to see an excellent service provided. But it also works within very tight budgets. There is a clash of interests. The householders want the shortest possible time between order and collection. The City does not want to go over budget. The more popular the service, the longer the wait time, the more scope for unhappy customers. The Council is in the business of managing down demand to save money, the householder wants an instant service. Bulky Bob's is caught in the middle, managing both sets of expectations.

There are also other hidden dangers in the large contract. If you don't like the gifts your partner bought for your birthday, you take them back and get your money refunded. As the

[5] www.liverpool.gov.uk

The degree of confidence in the service is inversely proportional to the distance from the frontline.

retailer, if your new range is unpopular you will know very quickly as you watch your sales plummet. Market reaction is swift and unambiguous.

In a public sector market it's more like an oil tanker turning. If your service is poor this may take some time to feedback to HQ. Once it does, you can then have a series of meetings with the council officer managing your contract. This can take many months. Unless there's an emergency, there isn't the pressure to keep the service quality high. And once the work goes out for re-tender, it may be too late and a competitor cleans up because of your tardiness in dealing with the slow decline of your service.

One way of dealing with this is to ensure that your managers and innovators stay close to the frontline and understand how the business feels at the point where your service connects with real live customers. The degree of confidence in the service is inversely proportional to the distance from the frontline. The further a manager is from it the front line, the better he or she believes the service is. So, stay close to your customers.

FRC has a programme called Walk A Mile. This requires anyone with supervisory and leadership responsibilities to regularly get on to the vehicles and into the shops to meet face to face the company's diverse range of customers. FRC has found it to be an invaluable process for ensuring customer service remains on top of the list of priorities and that timely changes are made to keep it there.

Bulky Bob's gets rave reviews and surpasses most of its targets. 60,000 plus collections a year running like clockwork. FRC is justifiably proud of it. Yet one manager returned from his day out with a crew quite worried. He described how a vehicle pulls up outside a customer's house to collect a fridge or three piece suite. Seeing the lorry – which has the legend 'Collects Recycles Restores' emblazoned in huge letters all over it – several other residents rush out and ask if "the lads" can take some other stuff away. They are refused. Cue sound of front doors slamming!

Now, the crews are doing what they have been told to by HQ. Demand must be managed and, if it's not on the list provided by the City's call centre, it doesn't get on the wagon. That is how the contract works and Bulky Bob's earns its money. All very sensible. Except if you are a resident not on the list, wanting to do your bit for recycling and you have a wardrobe cluttering up your kid's bedroom. To be refused makes no sense at all when there's a dirty great lorry idling in your street with three strapping men able to lift it on.

The manager worked out that this policy was creating over 5,000 annoyed non-customers a year. In one city! Time for a change. So a new system has been negotiated which is more flexible and manages out such potentially damaging unintended consequences.

Get real: beware wishful thinking

We need to be much better at differentiating between a social need and a market demand. Too often we see wishful thinking where hard headed realism should be.

It is perilously easy to confuse social need with market demand.

We visited a community café built with public money that was in serious financial trouble. It had seating for up to 60. On the parade of shops at the entrance to the estate was a well known private bakery and tea shop – which had seating for 8. Clearly there was a need for a community resource enabling people on the estate to get together in decent surroundings but not necessarily a demand for a large café. If there was a market demand for a 60 cover café, the chances are the private business would have expanded its space.

It is perilously easy – especially with so much under spent regeneration money around – to confuse social need with market demand or to believe that the community organisation's good intentions can create a market when the private sector company could not.

Don't kid yourself – if no-one is using the service it's not because they haven't heard enough about your fantastic vision its because they don't want it, at least not at the prices you are charging.

We see a lot of social enterprise plans where the sales projections can at best be described as "optimistic"! We notice that with public sector funders keen to spend their allocations, the sales lines in business plans do not get the rigorous questioning that, say, venture capitalists would give any plan looking to attract their money.

It is seductively easy to be over optimistic about future sales growth when it is "only" tax payers' money at stake. A really good test of any plan is to ask yourself: "Would I put my own money into this?" If a big part of you screams "no!" then you really do need to revisit the underlying assumptions and get real.

Managing Municipalities

doing business with the council

"If I had asked customers what they wanted they would have said a faster horse."
Henry Ford

F or any enterprise – social or otherwise – involved in social housing, employment, waste management and care services, dealing with the council is a fact of life. Many of the larger city authorities have at least a few social enterprise suppliers in waste management, care, furnishing or leisure services. Some are very well known such as ECT Recycling and Greenwich Leisure[1].

That the debate about the reform of public services now includes the possibility of the social enterprise model sitting alongside public and private sector options means that social enterprise has an opportunity. When a Cabinet minister jokes about Railtrack being run as a social enterprise and the social business model is talked about seriously as a way of running NHS services, it's clear that there is something significant going on. "We want to make it easier for social enterprises to win public procurement contracts", says the current minister with responsibility for social enterprise in the foreword to the DTI's impressive "toolkit" for social enterprises.[2] The social business is firmly in the Government's sights as a way of achieving its goals of improving public service provision.

But the Government's agenda and that of social enterprises are not identical. Be very careful. Making this opportunity work will involve managing the complex relationships which social enterprises have with public sector procurers. And it can be very challenging. "Interested in public contracts?", asks the DTI. "Have you thought through, and planned for, the potential risks to your organisation: over-expansion, performance failure, workforce issues and cash flow?". These are great questions which you ignore at your peril.

[1] www.gll.org   [2] www.dti.gov.uk/socialenterprise/news-toolkit.htm

When it works, the partnership between a local authority and a social enterprise can add a huge amount of value to the community. Great value can be added for both sides in the space created in the intersection between the council's goals for improved and more imaginative service delivery and the social business's desire to lock in income and scale up its social or environmental impact.

The partnership between FRC and Liverpool City Council underpins the huge success of Bulky Bob's, an FRC company that handles bulky household waste and is a model now being copied in other cities around the country. ECT Recycling has relationships with more than 20 local authorities and has become a leading innovator in recycling services. These are two of a handful of well known examples.

The extra costs of adding social value should be right out in the open and purchased from whoever can best deliver.

The potential benefits to the social enterprise of doing business with the public sector are obvious. The opportunity to scale up services and maximise impact, moving the organisation out of the margins and into the mainstream of the city's daily business. Solid contracts over a number of years, without the risk of bad debt, and creating a platform to innovate, diversify and grow.

As large and complex bureaucracies, local authorities are not easy partners for any company, large or small, social or private. Small, local private firms often feel as frustrated by council purchasing policies as social enterprises do, as they watch large companies clean up because they are easier for councils to manage.

We would like to see purchasers thinking about the linkages between the things they buy and the impact that can have on their wider objectives.

On the face of it, social enterprises should be well placed to benefit from an integrated procurement policy that seeks to achieve multiple policy goals. This is the market that social enterprises can go for but they will still have to compete and still have to show value.

The Best Value framework, a way of helping local authorities achieve the best overall deal in their procurement, does offer purchasers the tools to be more imaginative and to ask for social and environmental benefits.

We are not arguing for a special sheltered market for social enterprises. It is a demand side issue. We would like to see purchasers thinking about the linkages between the things they buy and the impact that can have on their wider objectives such as their regeneration and anti-poverty strategies. Such work would be available to any company that wants to bid – private or otherwise. This may encourage more collaboration between social and private enterprises as well as changing the way all businesses engage with public purchasers in the interests of service users and council tax payers.

For the social enterprise, supplier relationships can be even more complex and difficult to manage. There is a level of emotional investment by politicians in social enterprises in their wards and constituencies, and expectations, sometimes unfairly demanding, about what "their" social enterprises should or should not be doing.

Often middle ranking council employees do not share the high regard for social enterprise which politicians, with votes to win, do. Or there is no incentive to look for more creative ways of procuring services across departments for the city's residents. Politicians need to communicate the importance of joining up service improvements with their regeneration and social inclusion agendas and the opportunity that social enterprise may offer to the officers responsible for procurement.

Such partnering can bring brilliant results but it is very hard work and can put you and your social business in a very exposed position.

When the deal involves service delivery alongside, say, the recruitment and training of unemployed people, the management of that contract will mean that the social business must interact with different parts of the city council – waste management and regeneration for example. Whilst they might meet up at the top, the two departments may have different objectives and probably a different culture. You can find yourself in the bizarre position of having to explain to one part of the council what another is doing and helping them manage *their* systems so that you can successfully manage *your* business!

Says one social enterprise chief executive about his council customers: "Our relationship is weird. Dysfunctional but we need each other".

So, whatever the party politics involved or the local specifics, partnering public bodies brings extra challenges, which absorb management time and energy which no-one will ever pay you for or even think of paying you for. Such partnering can bring brilliant results when it works, the old win-win, but it is very hard work and can put you and your social business in a very exposed position. Be ready for that. When news of a successful bid came through, a social enterprise chief executive, acknowledging the mixed blessings of being in partnership with the local authority, was heard to say: "The good news is we got the contract. The bad news is we got the contract!".

The threat of a good example

Success also brings its own political dangers for your social enterprise and the wider sector. This 'Threat of a Good Example' cuts in two ways.

The leader of a very well known social business – let's call her Ms X – received a phone call one day. It was a prominent clergyman who had just come back from chairing a large meeting of the voluntary sector. It had gathered with all its hopes, fears, resentments, and competing agendas, to hear about the council's future grant funding plans. During a heated exchange, a senior politician said "why can't you all be more like X – she doesn't come to me all the time with her hand out." Ms X's social business has been championed vigorously by this councillor. The clergyman informed her that the meeting got very heated indeed after this intervention with much muttering about Ms X and her business! "What should we do," Ms X asked, "stop being successful and good at marketing ourselves?"

So, calling all politicians! Do not use successful social businesses as excuses to cut your grant aid to other organisations. Equally, be very careful if you are purchasing from social enterprises which are offering a cheaper service because they can attract sources of finance not available to private sector businesses. It might look like value for money locally but if the other source of finance is still public, your decision does not necessarily offer value for money to the tax payer.

Social enterprise is not compulsory and should never be made so. Don't forget that fundraising, maximising the use of volunteers, and all the other skills employed by voluntary and community organisations, need to be supported and acknowledged. They are assets as valuable to your city as the most successful and high profile of your social businesses.

It's also important to make sure that social enterprise is not being used as a cheap option. A major recycling social business did not get a service agreement in place at the start of its deal with the local authority in 1992, and has not achieved one since. The conservative estimate of the cost to the local authority, if the business had not provided a constructive alternative day-service for an average of 20 people a day for the last 10 years, would be £1 million. It now receives £30,000 per annum under a 'partnership agreement' although there is still no agreement in writing. Savings to social services are at least £800,000, an enormous loss of investment opportunity for the business.

There is no divine right for social enterprises to be taken seriously by anyone.

Winning work

Read the council's corporate plan, talk to procurement officers about what they will need, try to get joint meetings to join up policy objectives, find out what you will need to do and what the procurement eligibility issues will be, start talking about joint ventures in advance of contracts being let.

There is no divine right for social enterprises to be taken seriously by anyone let alone hard pressed council officers with the Audit Commission and local politicians on their backs. To succeed you must approach the issue not from a position of "they must support my social enterprise – which bit of the council's work should they give me" but rather ask yourself: "what are the unique strengths and qualities of my business which can help the council solve some of its toughest service delivery, regeneration or social inclusion problems?".

Crossing the borders

*doing the deal with
the private sector*

"*If it's not fun what's the point.*"

Ben Cohen

n parts of the private sector there is a burgeoning desire/willingness to "do good". In the United States particularly – but increasingly here in the UK – there is a generation of young entrepreneurs as passionate about putting something back into their communities as they are about building successful businesses and piling up cash. Perhaps the best known is Jeff Skoll, the founder of eBay, whose foundation gets behind some of the USA's most innovative socially entrepreneurial activity. And his Skoll Centre at Oxford University has further raised the profile of social entrepreneurs from around the world[1].

Corporate Social Responsibility is big business amongst big businesses and social and environmental auditing is becoming more common – if still too rare – amongst corporations. But in a post-Enron and WorldCom era, we must inevitably be cautious about globalised companies' claims in this area. Even when it's working, there is a danger that a lot of what passes for corporate social responsibility is limited to top down philanthropy. A recent survey for the World Economic Forum still had the public's trust in business leaders next to last.

But, whilst it is true that social and private businesses are generally very different, they share some core characteristics – both are about enterprise, both inhabit the same communities and both involve people who, by and large, want to see social justice and equity. Both have the capacity to do good in the communities in which they do their business.

In the public and third sector worlds there are very mixed attitudes towards private sector businesses. For some, they are the ideological enemy, capitalists driven only by the blind pursuit of profit with no regard for people or the environment. For others, the private sector is a foreign country rarely visited or thought about. And for a very small, pragmatic

[1] www.sbs.ox.ac.uk

Social and private businesses inhabit the same communities and both involve people who want to see social justice and equity.

and opportunistic minority of social enterprises, private companies are potential and actual business partners.

From the other side of the border, private sector business reactions to the citizens of "not for profit land" include disinterest, misunderstanding and condescension. There are a few which identify a business opportunity and become quite passionate about social enterprise, enabling them to do good *and* do well.

Win Win

Collaboration with private companies can offer a good opportunity for increasing sales, mixing talents and market access, to develop new products and services. You need to be clear what you are selling and then go out and find businesses to do deals with. Find out about the businesses first, find people who have contacts with them or places where you could meet and develop relationships.

In 2002, the Eldonians signed a deal with David McLean's, a large private design and build company. Together they aim at winning large scale housing development work a long way from their home patch in north Liverpool. This took time and required a financial investment by the social business in order to close the deal. It is a winning proposition. The private company's scale and market presence, the social business's knowledge of community involvement and managing neighbourhoods.

What these entrepreneurs are doing is combining mutual self interest with clear social and environmental returns. If the social enterprise sector is to grow and make a real difference in the economy we must see more of these kinds of deals. There is much great social enterprise work and innovation going on in the public sector market. But there is a much bigger world out there for social businesses to engage with.

It is a winning proposition. The private company's scale and market presence, the social business's knowledge of community involvement and managing neighbourhoods.

Many private businesses, particularly the growing and innovative ones, do deals with other companies. The dynamic nature of modern markets, and the ever shortening product life cycle, also mean that businesses are increasing the number of partnerships, joint ventures and other close working arrangements.

Social enterprise is about using market solutions to solve social problems and creating a social and financial return on investment. It will be more successful if it can bring business to address these problems from the start. The alternative is to get results and then wait for competitors to arrive. Successful social enterprises have unique and invaluable market knowledge and skills which can be brought to potential private sector partners. Social

Successful social enterprises have unique and invaluable market knowledge and skills which can be brought to potential private sector partners.

enterprise isn't going to be able to solve all the problems by itself. But it can show the way for others to follow, bringing new products and services to its communities.

Businesses have not pulled out of poor communities because they wanted to. They have pulled out because there is no effective demand for their goods and services. The local family owned corner shop that closes down because it can't sell enough, isn't closing because the family can make better profits somewhere else. And the reason there isn't effective demand may also be because other larger businesses have been able to attract enough of the corner shop's customers to make it uncompetitive, though not providing a service to all the people that used to shop there.

So, there is a job for social enterprise to engage with and mobilise the talents and knowledge of private businesses to bring them back into local economies. The opportunities in under served markets has been explored in the United States and more recently considered in a UK context by Business in the Community.[2] This can be done as part of public initiatives to, for example, provide better housing, better education and better health but social enterprise has an important role to play.

[2] www.bitc.org

By positioning itself at the interface between the worlds of the private and public sectors, the social enterprise builds trust across sectors and helps it access people, resources, ideas, and markets which will help it grow, diversify and innovate. FRC has done a deal to provide logistics support to a private furnishing business. This brings in new revenue but, equally importantly, exposes the social enterprise to new technologies and ways of doing things which will inevitably feed into the rest of its activities.

Businesses of all shapes and sizes, from multinationals to local SME's, will be interested in doing deals if they can see clear benefits. There are deals to be made with suppliers, neighbours, competitors, businesses with similar values, people who relish challenges and more. Sometimes they will be motivated by short term financial return, at others they will be seeking a longer term impact where the return may be less easy to assess.

Private partners are in it for business advantage and will stay as long as the margins make it worthwhile to do so.

This kind of relationship building is challenging. Although interested, sometimes passionately so in the social returns, private partners are in it for business advantage and will stay as long as the margins make it worthwhile to do so. It is a very different culture to that of the public and voluntary sectors. Getting this wrong will mean that the potential benefits of working with businesses are lost.

The Ariel Trust provides training and placements for long term unemployed people within commercial radio stations[3]. In 1996, Ariel Trust was trying to develop the radio sector as part

[3] www.arieltrust.com

of the cultural strategy of its local authority. They were able to get senior people from the radio industry together who set out what kind of support they thought the industry would require. As a result of this process applications for public funding were made and approved.

Unfortunately, the funding applications were designed to meet local authority and not business needs and did not reflect the way the industry operated. And it didn't work. Worse, Ariel lost credibility with the private sector. That credibility has now been regained but it has taken several years. It has done so by focusing on the operational needs of the industry. Now Ariel's strong links with the commercial sector enable it to achieve its objectives and get unemployed people into employment in commercial radio.

From charity case to business case

Be careful.

The differences between private and social enterprises are real and the terms of engagement must be carefully worked out. We know a joint venture company which was set up as a company limited by shares with social enterprise and private sector directors, the idea being to maximise social benefits by pooling social and private sector expertise. The company is doing well, but no thanks are due to the board, which has spent its time arguing about Directors' remuneration, expenses, overcharging, voting procedures, and philosophical differences as wide as an ocean. Little time was spent on what the business is all about. The private sector people blame the social enterprise people, and vice versa. They got married without a proper courtship, not understanding each others' different values and expectations.

Clarity of purpose and values fit – the two key criteria for striking good deals with a private sector company.

The deal FRC has done with the Ben & Jerry's ice cream company lies at the other end of the spectrum. FRC has the first PartnerShop franchise deal outside of the United States[4]. This deal enables it to benefit from the revenue generated by a well known premium high street brand and to take on young people other employers won't give a start to. Ben & Jerry's increase market share in England and the huge amount of media coverage generated by the store's opening helped build the company's 'caring capitalism' brand.

Ben & Jerry's has a very mature and nuanced social engagement policy built up over a number of years. This made it easier for two very different businesses to begin talking and to agree a deal. But most importantly, there is a values fit between the two organisations. There is a shared commitment not only to making money but to the social purpose. And these commitments are spelled out in a legally binding contract. Clarity of purpose and values fit – the two key criteria for striking good deals with a private sector company. Both companies are also committed to social reporting. Ben & Jerry's – perhaps uniquely – has managed to fuse its business interests and corporate social responsibility with the business interests and social agendas of its social enterprise partners like FRC.

---

[4] www.benjerry.com/scoop-shops/partnershops

The deal done between electrical retailer Dixons and Create involved a lot more trauma. Alan Uren is Managing Director of Business Services for the Dixons Group[5]. He got involved with the development of Create in Tottenham.

But its birth was painful. Says Alan: "The mistake we made was not listening and looking hard enough at what the differences are between the cultures of private business and the social enterprise. We thought, how hard can this be? We do big retail outlets selling white goods. This is just another one with some funny money from these regeneration bodies involved."

The Dixons people didn't grasp fully the triple bottom line culture which sees the quality of training and the positioning of the business in its community as every bit as important as retail sales levels. This led to tensions between them and Create's people. At heart this was about how Dixons – a huge complex company – perceived Create. They didn't see Create as a potential solution to their white goods disposal problems. "We didn't see that early enough", reflects Alan, "It was read across our company as a charitable thing unconnected to the 'real' business – a community affairs matter disconnected from our day to day operational realities and challenges".

But the lesson has been well learned and Alan has driven through a national deal with Create and Remploy[6] which has put in place the country's first national sortation and recycling network through which retailers solve their disposal problems and social businesses can exploit the waste stream. Create gets paid for clearing Dixons distribution centres of returned white goods thereby not only generating a revenue stream but getting its hands on

[5] www.dixons-group-plc.co.uk   [6] www.remploy.co.uk

a source of high volume, higher quality stock to refurbish and pass on. Dixons get a business problem solved, a better service and a good story about their commitment to greening the high street.

Alan again: "We now get that the private/social enterprise partnership can really be good for all of us. We have to put in place a deal which no matter what my successor thinks about social enterprise, he or she will support because it's good for our business. It's not a business-to-charity relationship but a business-to-business one".

And the deal has been great for Create. In Liverpool, the quantity and quality of stock received from Dixons distribution centres has led directly to increased production, higher sales levels and new jobs.

Reclaim's experience is somewhat less profitable. For a while, this social enterprise was flattered by the attention of big players in recycling like the old British Steel, under various new names. They sold Reclaim steel cans, and then bought them back as baled steel cans. Wasn't that nice? They were ever so friendly about it. Reclaim brought in a new commercial manager, and he was amazed at how much they were paying for raw material, and how little they were getting for their beautifully made bales. He asked senior officials in the steel industry why they were being squeezed at both ends, and was told - 'we thought you were a charity!'. They get a better deal now.

Crossing the borders

A good place to start if you want to more systematically engage with the private sector will be through your supply chain. Most of your suppliers will be private companies, probably of all shapes and sizes. How much do they know about your social agenda and aspirations? Spend time developing those relationships so that they value your business. You may find a new business opportunity for you by doing a rigorous analysis of your supply chains. One social enterprise we know which employs people with disabilities, use taxis to bring them to and from work to ensure they arrive on time and leave on time. You might not think that leaving on time is so important – but it is to the individuals concerned, and to the foreman who has the duty of locking up. Although the taxis are well paid on long term contracts, they rarely arrive on time. Many, many times they have arrived an hour or an hour and a half late. When asked for an explanation, one taxi firm replied 'it doesn't matter, does it – they're handicapped aren't they!' The only answer is to take this lucrative business away from them, and create a social enterprise. Watch this space!

Read the business press. See what companies are out there with whom you might be able to start a conversation. If you are committed to learning and innovation your paths will definitely cross with potential private partners. FRC would never have heard of the Ben & Jerry's PartnerShop if some of their people hadn't gone to the United States on a Cat's Pyjamas adventure.

Make it a partnership of equals where rewards and risks are fairly shared.

In the end, it will happen if you want it to happen. If your ideas are strong enough and your enterprise robust enough, you will attract private business who would be soft not to want to do business with you. But make it a partnership of equals where rewards and risks are fairly shared.

113

Being an alchemist

thriving through innovation

"If the world is changing faster outside your organisation than inside the end is near."

Jack Welch

W hat *If!* is an innovation company that offers its private sector clients this definition:

Innovation = insight + ideas + impact

To innovate is not simply to understand that there is the need for change or difference. Nor is it just being inventive and creative. It's both the passion and the ability to turn insights and ideas into meaningful action in the real world[1].

What *If!*'s blue-chip clients spend a huge amount of money and the time of their best people to think, create, invent and bring new products to market as fast as possible so they can grow and make more money.

They realise that in the information age, a good idea and some passion can outflank the most successful market leader. Why didn't Nescafé come up with the Starbucks idea? How come Stelios was able to come in under the noses of the big carriers and revolutionise a big part of the industry in Europe? Only with hindsight do Starbucks and easyJet's propositions seem so obvious.

"Industry revolutionaries invent new business models," says business guru Gary Hamel[2]. He cites IKEA, eBay, Nokia, Red Bull, easyJet, Dell Computer, and Wal-Mart as heretics who dare to challenge conventional wisdom about what business is and can do. Nokia used to make Wellington boots, Tesco now challenges the financial services industry. Such companies Hamel celebrates as "the ravaging winds of creative destruction".

[1] www.whatif.co.uk [2] www.garyhamel.com

Hotbeds of heresy, energy, creativity and relentless innovation –
revolutionaries inventing new social business models.
Is that your view of social enterprises?

Yet over time even the most successful business starts to lose it. Says Hamel: "Every business model loses its economic effectiveness. Markets get saturated, strategies get imitated, customers get more powerful, and good ideas get trumped by better ideas. To sustain success, a company must be capable of occasionally unhitching itself from the fading fortunes of its business model. Renewal requires an act of creative reconstruction in which assets are repurposed, competencies recombined, and human energies redirected". These words do not just apply to companies where shareholder value rules. Social enterprises must constantly be looking for ways to renew themselves, bringing forward better products and services to support their clients, customers and beneficiaries.

You would expect that the people dealing with the hard issues which the public and private sectors cannot resolve would be – would have to be – hotbeds of heresy, energy, creativity and relentless innovation – revolutionaries inventing new social business models. Is that your view of social enterprises? In all the strategies, documents, networks, policy forums, partnerships, you'll hear loads about funding, enabling environments, and the rest. But next to nothing about how we become a much more innovative sector.

Where are the social enterprise revolutionaries in the United Kingdom? For us, this goes to the heart of it. We can have the most locally owned, democratic, co-operative, mutually based, employee owned, non-profit distributing company in the world – but if we are not attempting to be as creative, groundbreaking, and heretical about received wisdom as the likes of easyJet, Nokia and Tesco – really what's the point?

Thank you Starbucks, but getting people to drink more coffee is not one of humanity's most burning needs! Nice one Stelios, but making it cheaper to fly to Barcelona for a weekend is great but hardly a defining moment in civilisation's forward march. We like the new mobile phone technology as much as the next person but can live without being able to send pictures of ourselves by phone.

How often it is that we hang on to what we've got rather than take risks and try and create brilliant new ideas?

But how do we reduce inequality? How do we improve our communities? How can poor families' choices be increased? These are the important questions worthy of our best brains and creativity. And yet and yet. Too often those in the welfare and community development arenas – and those running social enterprises – are no quicker or more imaginative than those seeking to maximise shareholder value. How often it is that we hang on to what we've got rather than take risks and try and create brilliant new ideas?

Preparing this book, we sent out loads of emails asking for examples of social innovation, of new products and services being brought to under served markets and making a real difference in the lives of poor people and their communities.

The best examples we could find mainly came from overseas. Financial services to the rural poor of India and Bangladesh. Affordable and appropriate technology in Africa. We love Roundabout Outdoor in South Africa[3]. This brilliantly simple idea involves using children's roundabouts to power water pumps. Rural women who walk miles to get water no longer need to do the back breaking pumping. The kids do it whilst playing. It's simple, cheap, low tech and it works.

Why are so few of the Schwab Foundation's star social entrepreneurs UK based? Why does David Bornstein in his excellent book "How to Change the World" have to reach back in history to find his example of a British social entrepreneur? Guess who? Florence Nightingale! Perhaps in Third World contexts or in the USA, where poverty is so much more widespread and the state more distant or weak, there is more scope for social innovation than in the countries of the European Union where the culture of state welfare is deep rooted. The space for social innovation may well be smaller and more complicated here but we must learn from the sometimes breathtaking ambition of people such as Muhammad Yunus.

The problems besetting our communities may not be of the scale and acuteness of India or Colombia but they are real nonetheless and there is much to be done. We believe that the creativity required to regenerate a community on a run down British housing estate blighted by drugs, crime and alienation, is every bit as challenging as getting micro finance to women in rural India.

If you are active in real markets – where your customers and beneficiaries can buy elsewhere – the pressure is on you to innovate so you can retain market share. If you are up against

[3] www.worldbank.org/afr/findings/english/find218.pdf

private businesses they will probably be more focused than you because, with only one bottom line, they can bring relentless attention to providing what the customer wants. This is true too for large corporates which get blindsided by smaller, faster moving innovators.

If your social enterprise runs contracts which arise from a competitive process and you are not innovating, the chances are you will lose work when it comes up for tender. ECT Recycling is a great example of how market pressures have created new and better services which, not only fuel ECT's impressive growth, but also bring environmental benefits and convenience to householders. And they are not stopping there. ECT now runs bus routes in London and is investigating how it might operate a train service.

Large scale growth like ECT's isn't the only way. Innovation can be spun out in new social enterprises. Create was spun out of FRC as a stand alone business, part of its wider family but free to find its own way.

Innovation can also result in a more cost effective way of providing the same service, freeing up resources to add value. One thing is true, the world doesn't stop changing and much of the change is widening the gap between rich and poor which only adds to the pressure for change.

One option, perhaps the easiest, in so far as any innovation is ever easy, is process innovation – that is, improving the way in which a product is made in order to free up resources to do something else. How often are you reviewing your business processes on the hunt for how you can make them better and more responsive to your customers?

Another option is to deliver the same product into a new market, expanding by rolling out the business model to new areas. Community Action Network is doing some interesting work on franchising and replication[4]. But transplanting the success of a social enterprise born in one city or region into another is no easy task and few have succeeded.

Another option is to provide a new product into an existing market. Faced with increased competition and a fast changing market, FRC has had to invent new services. Where once its customers had only one choice – buy the furniture or don't – they can now rent it, lease it, have FRC manage the stock or move it around from property to property as demand dictates. The breaking up of public housing stock into smaller units inspired FRC to bring a removals business to market – A Moving Experience – which is growing quickly, adding value to tenants and opening up new revenue streams for FRC.

Bulky Bob's was an idea that FRC took to an existing local authority customer. An idea that proposed adding value to an existing service. The idea was supported but it still took three years to get from idea to launch. Partly this is about getting the customer to see you in a different light and partly it's about getting them to see services in a different way. But getting new products to market can take more time than you think, especially when you are selling into the public sector.

The toughest nut to crack, but the one that offers the highest potential returns, is to sell new products into new markets. This means going to people that you do not have a relationship with and persuading them that they urgently need to buy something from you that they

[4] www.can-online.org.uk

haven't seen before and is untested. How many times have you heard people say they want innovation and then say 'do you know anywhere else where this is being tried?'

When we had the idea for the Cat's Pyjamas we could have spent time and money on market research and consulted widely. But we didn't. We simply put an advert in the paper to gauge demand. There was and it grew from there. The big advantage of selling to the general public is that your income comes from large numbers of small contracts. Okay, so the Cat's Pyjamas is not capital intensive so the risk was small, but the point is that, whatever the business, at some point you have to move from research to action and back your hunch.

How many times have you heard people say they want innovation and then say 'do you know anywhere else where this is being tried?'

At some point in all this innovation, the issue of intellectual property will arise. Intellectual property is just as important for a social enterprise as it is for any other business. The organisation needs to be able to internalise these property rights in order that it can exploit them to further its achievement of a double bottom line. Intellectual property has a current or potential future value that represents an income stream. Find it and protect it.

Not all innovative ideas work. Organisations will invest time and money from reserves, take ideas to market and fail. The organisation needs to know when to stop but also needs to support the team that put together the product. If you are not having failures now and again you can't be taking risks or innovating.

*Take some calculated risks, celebrate your successes,
learn from failure, and never give up.*

So, begin today to build a culture of creativity and innovation inside your social business which involves everyone from board to shop floor. Get out there, learn and be inspired by the best of the private and social enterprise worlds. Stay close to your customers, put time, money and energy into innovation. Take some calculated risks, celebrate your successes, learn from failure, and never give up.

All change please!
what happens when you grow?

"Here's a cold hard reality for you: at any given time your business can only be going one of two ways. Up. Or Down."

Sahar and Bobby Hashemi

It is commonly believed that growth is a good thing. The Inner City 100 awards celebrate and reward it[1]. It's a good thing if a business reports that last year it turned over £200,000 and employed 13 people. This year it's £350,000 and 21 people. We serviced 736 clients last year, we will see over 1,000 this year. 23,000 fridges refurbished then, 47,000 now. Good things.

Well, hang on there. Is growth in itself a good thing? Should all social enterprises go for it? We don't think so. An unexamined, un-thought through pattern of growth can be a very bad thing indeed. Large organisations are not just big small ones (if you know what we mean!) and the social enterprise which grows, without having clearly decided that this is what it really wants, and what impact there will be on it, will probably hit the wall.

Let's not make growth a virtue in itself. It's not obligatory. Very few private companies grow beyond half a dozen people. And growth is no indication that a social enterprise is achieving its purposes. All it means is that it is getting bigger. In fact, the chances are, the faster you grow the greater the risk that the quality of your social return will deteriorate. You may be refurbishing more fridges for poor families but unexamined growth may mean that the failure rate of the appliances is increasing and fewer people on your training programme are graduating to a job. The value of social accounting to track the quality of the social and environmental impacts is critical during growth, although it is more difficult to do it then because it will seem like a luxury when the operational issues of a growing business demand precedence. And yet it creeps up on you and can then set off with an irresistible momentum.

[1] www.theinnercity100.org

*The social enterprise which grows without having clearly decided
that this is what it really wants will probably hit the wall.*

We have seen too many great little enterprises get spoiled by growing without really thinking about it. The quality of the service dives because management energy is diverted into keeping the pay roll funded. Maintenance of the organisation becomes the priority not innovation or enhancing service and product.

And, as you grow, you have to specialise. This posed a particular problem for Rubicon Enterprises in San Francisco where they employed social workers on the social side and entrepreneurs to do the deals. Rubicon's Rick Aubry: "The social workers thought they were only interested in profit and the entrepreneurs thought that the social workers could not do math. The "profitable" parts resented subsidising "loss" making parts even though the social profit was the main objective".

The growing social enterprise, or the grant funded enterprise trying new sales strategies, will face the same issues as a private company: cash flow problems; the risk of over trading; logistics headaches; and recruitment and retention nightmares. But the issue we want to focus on here is what can be learned about the challenges to organisational culture which have been faced by social businesses which have made the leap from grants to sales and have grown to scale.

Staying small and local is honourable. But so too is acknowledging that you're good at what you do, so why not do more of it? Be ambitious. ECT, according to award winning social entrepreneur and CEO Steve Sears, was up for it from the beginning: "We deliberately pursued a 'growth at all costs' strategy in order to spread our overheads and risks".

ECT's business success – £20 million, 600 employees – speaks for itself. But it is unusual in having got to such scale from very local roots in west London.

Go for growth but with your eyes wide open.

Paul Harrod and his team at Aspire were really put through the wringer when the business was hit by a major cash flow crisis in 2003. The business experienced dramatic growth over a couple of years, including the setting up of half a dozen regional independent enterprises distributing the catalogue and supporting homeless people. Says Paul: "We grew too quickly without really thinking through the consequences. There were all sorts of pressures on us, commercial and political, to go big fast. Not many social enterprises had done this before and we had no-one to advise us properly from a position of experience. We should have road tested the business model before committing large resources and time to a national roll out."

As Aspire's profile as a nationally significant social enterprise grew, they built a national structure which, in the heat of the moment, made sense. "We should have tried harder to learn from others before committing ourselves to such growth", Paul acknowledges. So when a major cash problem hit, the company's complex dispersed structure was unable to respond quickly enough. The lack of flexibility and inability to take fast decisions, which would be uniformly implemented, added to the company's money worries.

Aspire's response to its problems has been robust and imaginative, involving a wide range of stakeholders. The company's leadership has swallowed its medicine and its restructure has attracted new investment. Re-modelling continues, but sales are on an upward curve and the future looks better for the business, the homeless people and Third World producers who benefit – but it was high anxiety for a while there. "We learned the hard way", reflects Paul, "but I don't regret doing it. The social benefits of employing homeless people have been significant".

FRC experienced dramatic growth in the late nineties. It was far from easy. Barry Mckenzie, one of the few board members who survived the dramatic shift from fundraised charity to social business, observed the growing pains: "The mid to late nineties was a very challenging period for us. I don't think we grasped the impacts of the culture change that was a going on. We were just trying to stay in business but something a lot more profound was happening. Not realising this meant that we forgot what it might be doing to the people on the frontline."

Relying on fundraised income and surviving by selling are two very different things. The ways you generate income shape your culture, the types of people you need, the way everything works. Says Barry: "It became painfully clear that we had great people but they were doing the wrong jobs now. Things were changing so quickly people were pushed to their limits and sometimes beyond. And there was trouble at board level with different staff members' champions disagreeing."

This had a profound effect on relationships and there are people who were great friends who now don't speak to each other. In truth, there was a civil war at senior management level. Alongside the huge skills and experience gaps which opened up, there were unresolved differences of opinion about the wisdom of going for sales income and the way it was being done. "I don't for a second regret that we went down the social business road," says Barry. "It has been great for us and the people we were created to serve. But we were perhaps naive in thinking that the people we had were the people who could take us into a different future".

His advice to any social entrepreneurs considering the transformation of their organisations? "It won't be easy. Expect a lot of turbulence. But over everything, make sure you have your people behind you, understanding what it is you're trying to do. And know that you will be a completely different entity by the time you've finished".

Our sector likes to think of itself as fairly radical and brave. But let's be honest.

Jerr Boschee is an experienced and trenchant analyst of what it takes to run a social business. He warns his clients who want to change and grow that it won't be easy: "Culture eats change for breakfast and any non-profit that hopes to become entrepreneurial, regardless of whether it is starting a business venture or pursuing earned income opportunities within its programs, must undergo a radical set of changes".

Our sector likes to think of itself as fairly radical and brave. We're committed to change and The People, aren't we? We're not like those horrible people in state structures who thwart us or the private sharks who are only in it for the money. But let's be honest. We can be as change resistant, reactionary, conservative and slow moving as the most bureaucratic council or autocratic owner manager.

You will need therefore to make sure you have the people in your teams and board willing to move into this brave new world or that you can get them.

No doubt there are enterprises out there where the change from grants to sales has gone like clockwork and quick large scale growth has been pain free. The results of getting to scale and profitability are there for all to see in the work of such pioneers as ECT, FRC, Big Issue and the rest. But our advice is to think long and hard about it before trying to join them and make sure you learn from what happened to them. You'll make your own mistakes. You don't need to make theirs!

ALL CHANGE, PLEASE!

THE
HOLY BIBLE
—
DOUAY VERSION

And nothing
but the truth

but how can you be sure?

"No legacy is as rich as honesty."

William Shakespeare

So, here are all these people, the social entrepreneurs and social business managers, board members, funders and investors, working hard to balance this triple bottom line, continually innovating and dealing with constant change. But how do any of them know if it's working?

How can anyone really know if and what effect their social enterprise is having? How can we know if our social and environmental purposes and objectives are being met? How do we prove it?

By social reporting, that's how! By gathering, assessing and distributing independently verified data and feedback which is honest and understandable.

Verifying the financial bottom line is easy. There are universally accepted protocols, backed by legislation, which mean that we can read a company's annual audited accounts and get reliable information about its financial performance. This enables us to make informed decisions about whether we'd invest in, trade with, work for or buy from this particular organisation.

But there is no equivalent framework for us to draw conclusions about a social enterprise's social and environmental impact. With some notable exceptions, the truth is that most claims made by social enterprises round the world about their efficacy, are based upon aspiration and subjective impressions. Too often the value of the social enterprise intervention is taken for granted and our claims not robustly interrogated. There is often some gathering of data around job outcomes or numbers of people helped but too little about quality, still less an independently audited analysis of impacts.

It is claimed that some things just cannot be measured or quantified, such as improved quality of life or changes in attitude amongst long term unemployed people. We don't buy this but we do acknowledge that social reporting is as much an art as a science and that creativity is required to find ways of uncovering and articulating the complexities of personal and social change.

There are some other things which are also true. It is a field littered (and we mean littered) with jargon. Social accounting (the process of gathering the data and feedback). Social auditing (done by an external auditor to verify the soundness of the data and its sources). Social reporting (letting everyone know what the accounts have found and drawing interpretations from them). Sustainability reporting (another name for social and environmental reporting). Stakeholder engagement (communicating with the range of people – staff, customers, suppliers – who really matter to your business). Perhaps because of the jargon, social reporting it is still very much a minority interest.

Social reporting is as much an art as a science and creativity is required to find ways of uncovering and articulating the complexities of personal and social change.

Surprisingly, most of the companies featured in this book do very little systematic analysis of their social impacts. The profile of social reporting has risen a bit over the last couple of years but there is no sign of an upsurge of interest in the sector.

Beyond a few big corporates – such as Co-op Bank, Shell, BP – social and environmental reporting hardly exists in the private sector and there is huge scepticism within the corporate world – let alone the anti-globalisation movement – about its purposes and value.

We should be setting the standards and showing the private sector how it's done. But the evidence is not there yet.

Surely the social business, whose very reason for existing is to create social and environmental benefit, would see social reporting every bit as important as financial accounting or HR. We should be setting the standards and showing the private sector how it's done. But the evidence is not there yet.

We are passionate advocates of social reporting and our purpose in this chapter is to encourage you to get involved with it. There are three reasons why social reporting is a must-do.

Firstly, done well, social reporting will make your social enterprise a better business and enhance the quality of your social impacts. The social accounting process requires data gathering and assessment systems to operate across your business. This will provide you with golden intelligence about what is actually going on in your organisation and how it is viewed externally. If you act in a timely and positive way, this will improve your business, make you more responsive to your customers and make it more likely you will keep them.

Secondly, it can prove your worth to the people who matter to you – your stakeholders – and so build trust in you and your social business. FRC, a leader in this field, has found that by offering its public sector customers access to the data it gathers from, for example, tenants, it has built confidence with them and increased its chances of winning repeat business and cross selling.

Thirdly, we believe there is a moral responsibility to do social reporting. Most social enterprises have access to free development money – from foundations, the Lottery and so on – which is unavailable to small private businesses. Private firms also must pay corporation tax and full business rates. Many social enterprises are exempt from most of this. We have dealt earlier with the issues of subsidy – or, rather, compensation – but the point to make here is that if the tax payer provides social businesses with access to free money and tax breaks in order to help them achieve their social purposes, then surely there is an obligation to strive to demonstrate what is being achieved by the use of that money?

At our events, we have heard it said that whilst social reporting may have the beneficial effects we claim, it is too much work for a small organisation and too difficult to do from a standing start. We disagree. Most organisations already gather a lot of information and some of it ends up in reports to various stakeholders. So you will probably be well on the way.

"At its heart it is really simple. It is also very easy to over complicate it and make it harder than it needs to be."

Of course, there will be challenges as you roll social reporting out across the business, but it's important not to lose sight of these basics. Alison Ball at FRC is one of the country's leading thinkers and practitioners on making social accounting a reality inside real life businesses: "At its heart it is really simple. It is also very easy to over complicate it and make it harder than it needs to be. The biggest issue we had to overcome was staff scepticism and their false beliefs that this would make their jobs more difficult". Alison says that it has taken about three years of concerted effort to get social reporting embedded in the company's culture. "The big swing point was when the commercial people in the business understood that they'd be better and win more work by using the data we were gathering."

Perhaps uniquely, FRC produces monthly management accounts with a literal triple bottom line, providing managers and board with financial, social and environmental data in the same report. This includes information from gross profit margins, to numbers of homes furnished, to CO_2 emissions.

Your report provides another way of communicating with customers and beneficiaries so reinforcing your brand. You might even win an award.

Getting started

Keep it simple and straightforward. Don't oppress yourself by trying quickly to go from nothing to a bells and whistles system. Small, under resourced organisations need to focus on the areas where the link between their social objectives and the financial results is most obvious. Money is always tight for what is seen – mistakenly in our view – as non-essentials like reporting, so go to where the impact will be clear soonest.

The most important thing is to set out your values, making sure that everyone in the organisation understands them and then set out your objectives. This will be the framework against which you can report. And, again, the simpler and clearer the better.

Stakeholders – the people who matter

The next thing to do is work out who is effected by or can effect your organisation and to sort out what you should be asking them and when.

Talking and listening to the people your business works with and employs is just good business and it's the only way you can understand what impacts you're having. A formal approach to this process, stakeholder engagement, provides you with useful information that is relevant to your business. Easy enough to list the people you have an impact on although even here you can miss people out. Harder to assess what information you want from them, how much you need for it to be useful and then getting to them, possibly through surveys, focus groups, phone calls, one to one interviews.

Once you start thinking this way, you'll be amazed at just how many peoples' lives your enterprise actually touches – as customers, employees, trainees, directors, suppliers, funders, investors, visitors, and neighbours.

If you are going to take decisions on the basis of all this listening, you need to make sure that you talk to enough people for the information to be meaningful.

When London's Bootstrap Enterprises[1] began supporting new business start ups, seeking entrepreneurs from deprived communities, it provided accommodation, finance and advice and did well. An evaluation reported cost per job of between £3,000 and £5,000. Excellent. But then came the soul searching. The business survival rate was low and the job output indicator was not a good measure of success. Bootstrap was tending towards selecting people who they thought would do better in business and excluding others. But the people involved *were* going on to get good jobs in London.

As Bootstrap talked to the people who had been through the programme, it had to ask whether it was an effective approach to put people in situations where the new business could fail even if they went on to other things. Certainly it was having a negative impact on staff.

[1] www.bootstrap-enterprises.org

The organisation changed its focus to run business development training, focusing on the elements of their programmes from which people benefited during their experience of running a business. And it worked. 30% went on to jobs with living wages, 30% did then start their own business and a third went on to further education.

Not everyone wanted to start a business. Many wanted a good job. And, most importantly, in London there are a lot of jobs. Not necessarily new jobs, often the focus of regeneration programmes. But vacancies in existing jobs. Asking the right questions of the right people, led to big changes.

FRC has been experimenting with and refining its employee engagement work for a number of years. One of its social objectives is to be a great place to work, creating a supportive and empowering environment for all its people. But it doesn't always get the questions right. One year they wanted to find out why people were staying so long at FRC. Why was staff turnover so small? One of the questions workers were asked was "Are you paid enough for the job you do?" A large number of respondents ticked the "No" box. One to one interviews following up the questionnaire, revealed that the question people thought they were being asked was "Do you want more money?" The next year, the question was refined so that the intention was unambiguous: "Have you seen a job like yours advertised over the last six months offering more money than you are on at FRC?" So be careful of the language you use. Having an external auditor will also help with this. FRC's auditor JustAssurance[2] also offers their client advice on the process, as well as verifying the outcomes of the accounting systems.

[2] www.justassurance.org.uk

Indicators of success

Now you are in a position to measure progress against your objectives and compare how you are doing with other organisations.

You can compare how much money you made with other organisations and with your last year's results. With social objectives that is not so easy. There is always lot of debate about finding indicators and the trick is choosing the right ones for you.

Create is a social business refurbishing and selling white goods and offering salaried training for the long term unemployed. There is an impact on productivity when working with long term unemployed people which was particularly difficult for Create as they were selling their products, the refurbished white goods, in the open market in competition with a number of private businesses.

A key issue was how much was it costing the organisation in lost productivity compared with private operators and, as importantly, how much should it be costing in a well run organisation. An assessment of the business several years ago, highlighted an industry average productivity rate of 4 white goods recycled per person per day, compared with the 1 per person per day that Create was achieving and suggested a target of between 1 and 2 per person per day. Given the previous unemployment history of Create's trainees, a lower productivity was to be expected.

But who was going to pay for this lost productivity when there was no way the price of the product could be increased? Create had a contract with a public employment agency. On paper, in terms of cost per trainee, it looked expensive. Even when taking into account the cost of the difference in productivity achieved compared with private sector competitors, it still looked expensive.

But this wasn't the right comparison. There are at least three other important factors in salaried training schemes; how long people have been unemployed, how many get jobs and how long those new jobs last. Whilst there were no nationally accepted rules for taking these factors into account, a new cost per person in employment, weighted for the period of unemployment and the length of the new job showed that the cost was more than comparable with other schemes. Enlightened organisations are now building in systems to track people after they leave the training programme.

One word of warning whilst you're counting up all the positive impacts you have had. In social economy circles, the positive social impacts of private businesses can be forgotten. You may employ long term unemployed people but so do many businesses. You may provide services to your community but so do many local businesses. So your performance needs to be assessed in relation to private businesses, as well as other social enterprises.

Accounting systems

Have you ever asked a member of your staff if everything is okay only to find out a few days later that everything is far from okay and a big hole has opened up in front of you? It is important to establish robust and accurate systems for gathering the data upon which you will make decisions, which may mean changing course or jettisoning projects altogether.

FRC had a number of training contracts but did not have the right systems in place for monitoring contract performance, numbers of trainees, costs per trainee, and allocation of overhead costs. The company believed everything was fine. But, an external audit highlighted a lack of evidence to support the grant payment and the organisation ended up making an unbudgeted and possibly unnecessary repayment.

You may think this is just about internal management systems but it goes straight to the heart of a social audit. Progress against an objective to train unemployed people can only be confirmed by reference to records of attendance, exam results, job support and destinations.

Reporting to your stakeholders

It's all very well having this information on the impact you have on your stakeholders and your performance against your objectives, but, if it isn't being used, it isn't very useful. The organisation should account for its performance to all its stakeholders, responding to their issues so that they can make informed decisions. Perhaps the single most important part of this process is how you respond to the issues raised. If you never change as a result of the social audit process then there is probably something wrong.

But how honest can you be? A commitment to transparency and honest reporting might be a double edged sword waiting to cut you. Your competitors will certainly be interested. The main competitor of one large social business used the honesty of its report to bad mouth it to customers. When you are competing for contracts with businesses that do not produce social reports, let alone have them independently verified, having your social audit report on your website might not help you. An enlightened customer might think 'how honest of them' but they might not, and your honesty loses you points with procurers playing it by the book.

This is a risk that social enterprises must face whilst developing prospective customers' understanding of the social audit process.

An enlightened customer might think 'how honest of them' but they might not and your honesty loses you points with procurers playing it by the book.

Verification

Your report can build trust amongst the people you effect, especially those outside the organisation, your customers and your neighbours, and getting it independently verified will help. Having someone from outside your organisation test your conclusions will also help improve your business. How you do this can range from organising a panel of people who know about your business through to retaining an independent auditor to report on your report, in much the same way as a financial auditor.

A discipline of integrity

We've tried our best to make this chapter as interesting and readable as possible and not sound too much like social accounting anoraks!

We are passionate about this and we have to acknowledge that we sometimes feel like voices crying in the wilderness! And, we have to acknowledge that the value of social accounting remains unproven. The experiences of leaders in the field like FRC – in 2002 the first social enterprise winner of the ACCA/Accountability Best Social Report[3] – is that the evidence of its effectiveness is contradictory. Its honesty and transparency has done it no favours in some of its public sector markets, where acknowledging mistakes leaves you open for procurers to mark you down. But with its private sector partners, its independently verified report offers a degree of comfort about the real results of its activities. Of course, they may have gone ahead with FRC with or without a social report.

[3] www.acca.co.uk   www.accountability.org.uk   www.frcgroup.co.uk

Yes, social reporting will give you invaluable data about your impact. It will definitely strengthen and mature your business systems. It may win you new work.

We believe that part of being a social enterprise is to seek to prove the value of our social and environmental interventions. It is one of the differentiators between the social and the private business. Without a social report what value can any claims about the efficacy of the social enterprise business model have?

In the end, it is a discipline of integrity.

AND NOTHING BUT THE TRUTH

"For anyone who has said, "this isn't working" or "We can do better!" – for anyone who gets a kick out of challenging the status quo, shaking up the system or practicing a little entrepreneurial "creative destruction" – these are propitious times."

David Bornstein

And finally . . .

For the pessimist there is no shortage of data. A report, released at the World Economic Forum on 15 January 2004, concludes that governments, business, international organisations and civil society are doing only one third of what they should be to realise the United Nations Millennium Declaration goals. In 2000, leaders of 189 countries committed themselves to a set of actions to address poverty, hunger, the environment, education and human rights, with a deadline of 2015. A panel of independent analysts concludes that in none of these areas is the international community scoring more than 4 out of 10. No problems though in finding billions of dollars and pounds to invade Iraq. The disconnect between those in cabinet and board room, and the mass of the people, particularly the poor, seems wider than ever.

And yet, our work through the Cat's Pyjamas, and the privilege it affords of us of meeting and connecting with social entrepreneurs and social enterprise leaders from all over the world, gives us huge encouragement. Whether it's Trevor Muluadzi, sorting out the toilets in South Africa's schools; Claire Dove creating opportunities for Liverpool's marginalised women; Muhammad Yunus getting cash and technology to Asia's poor; Mimi Silbert

*How can we be pessimistic when there are people like this
all over the planet, full of passion, energy, creativity
and staying power?*

transforming the lives of ex-offenders in California – there is another world out there, which doesn't get on CNN all the time, and runs alongside big business as usual, showing how differently things can be done.

How can we be pessimistic when there are people like this all over the planet, full of passion, energy, creativity and staying power? The immovable object of global injustice defended by vested interests and the irresistible force of the growing movement of social entrepreneurs.

In this worldwide context, this nation's social enterprise conversation can be very inward looking and parochial. The truth is that to create the scale of change needed, we must not exclude the private sector from the conversation. But, by making "social enterprise" a noun, and not the description of an attitude – a state of mind – this is precisely what we have done in Britain.

So, for us, the point is not that we create lots more social enterprises of particular legal forms or that we have schools and hospitals run by social businesses. Our ambition should be bigger than that.

We believe that if we are to start to resolve the inequalities in our world, then we will have to find more people to take up the challenges. We must get better at learning from one another, building alliances between and across sectors, cultivating and strengthening that socially enterprising world view. The Cat's Pyjamas will continue to help that networking and learning happen. The really interesting conversations are happening at the border between private business and social entrepreneurs and it is there we will focus our attention.

These are exciting times.

Are you up for it?

References and acknowledgements

Page 33 *Social Enterprise in Anytown* ISBN 0 903319 97 7 Written by John Pearce and published by Calouste Gulbenkian Foundation.
Quote used with the kind permission of the publisher

Page 128 *Anyone Can Do It* ISBN 1 84112 204 1 Written by Sahar and Bobby Hashemi and published by A John Wiley and Sons Co.
Quote used with kind permission of the publisher

Page 154 *How To Change the World* ISBN 0 19 513805 8 Written by David Bornstein and published by Oxford University Press.

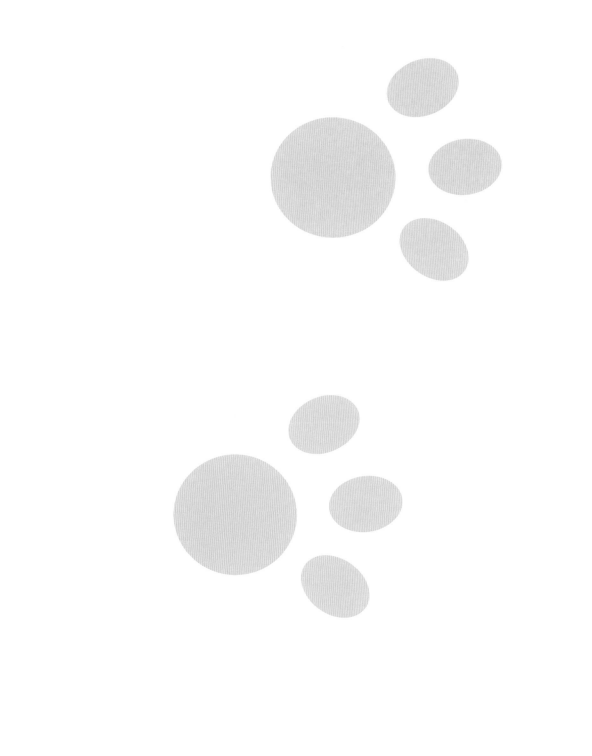

Liam Black

Liam Black is co-founder of the Cat's Pyjamas and one of the country's best known social entrepreneurs and social business leaders. A renowned speaker on social enterprise and organisational change, he has extensive leadership experience with high profile social businesses such as The Big Issue and the FRC Group. He is a founder director of Create and Create UK.

Jeremy Nicholls

Jeremy's work has taken him across Africa, Central America and the UK in public, private and voluntary organisations. In 1991 he escaped the accountancy profession to spend two years at home with his son before returning to 'work' and starting a consultancy business. He is the founder and director of two other businesses, one of which is the Cat's Pyjamas and he is currently the chair of AccountAbility.